HEALING GRIEF
AT WORK

Also by Alan Wolfelt:

Creating Meaningful Funeral Ceremonies:
A Guide for Families

Healing a Friend's Grieving Heart:
100 Practical Ideas for Helping Someone
You Love Through Loss

Healing a Teen's Grieving Heart:
100 Practical Ideas for Families, Friends
and Caregivers

Healing Your Grieving Heart for Kids:
100 Practical Ideas

The Journey Through Grief:
Reflections on Healing

Understanding Your Grief:
Ten Essential Touchstones For Finding
Hope and Healing Your Heart

When Your Pet Dies:
A Guide to Mourning, Remembering,
and Healing

Companion Press is dedicated to the education and support of both the bereaved and bereavement caregivers.

We believe that those who companion the bereaved by walking with them as they journey in grief have a wondrous opportunity: to help others embrace and grow through grief—and to lead fuller, more deeply-lived lives themselves because of this important ministry.

Companion
P R E S S

For a complete catalog and
ordering information, write or call:

Companion Press
The Center for Loss and Life Transition
3735 Broken Bow Road
Fort Collins, CO 80526
(970) 226-6050
www.centerforloss.com

HEALING GRIEF
AT WORK

•

100 PRACTICAL IDEAS AFTER YOUR
WORKPLACE IS TOUCHED BY LOSS

•

ALAN D. WOLFELT, PH.D.

Companion
PRESS

Fort Collins, Colorado
An imprint of the Center for Loss and Life Transition

Companion Press is an imprint of the
Center for Loss and Life Transition,
3735 Broken Bow Road, Fort Collins, Colorado 80526
(970) 226-6050

Companion Press books may be purchased in bulk for sales promotions, premiums or fundraisers. Please contact the publisher at the above address for more information.

Printed in the United States of America

11 10 09 08 07 06 05   5 4 3 2 1

ISBN: 1-879-651-45-9

To the executive team at Hallmark Cards who understood the need for a peer mentoring program called Compassionate Connections, in which employees who have experienced a life challenge support coworkers with similar crises in their lives—and to all enlightened employers large and small.

INTRODUCTION

Why the workplace is a grieving place

If there's been a death in your life, you get three days off work—and it had better be a biological, nuclear family member. Then it's chin up, carry on, back to work...

Imagine that living your life is like driving a car. Inside this car are seated all the various parts of your self—your family self, your physical self, your spiritual self, etc. Depending on where the car is going at any particular moment in your life, a different self needs to be in the driver's seat.

If you are reading a book with your child, your parental self is in the driver's seat. If you are grocery shopping, your task-oriented self is in the driver's seat. If you are playing a sport, your physical self is in the driver's seat. And so on.

At work, your work self is in the driver's seat. In a culture like ours where work is so highly valued and so much of our self-worth is tied up in our jobs, we tend to think of our work selves as one of the most important drivers in the car—sometimes *the* most important driver in the car. So when your work self has to concentrate on driving, all the backseat selves typically understand that it's time to hush up and maybe even take a nap.

But now—a death.

When someone you care about dies, a new and very high maintenance driver climbs into the car. Its name is grief. It may be sad and it may be angry and it is, without a doubt, relentless. And it wants to be in the driver's seat all the time, especially in the early weeks and months after the death.

Grief is not only taking over the car, it's affecting all the other selves in the car. It's causing your emotional self lots of distress. It's giving your physical self various aches and pains. It's rendering your cognitive self unable to concentrate. It's making your spiritual self question whether you ever want to go to work again and the very meaning of life.

And it even has the nerve to wrestle for the steering wheel with that work self of yours. During the workday, your work self is trying to drive and concentrate on the road, but it's having a hard time because that grief self is always either grabbing the wheel or squirming in the passenger seat, protesting and demanding your undivided attention.

So, whether you want the workplace to be a grieving place or not, reality suggests that it is.

The misconception about grief at work

There's a misconception about our feelings and work and it goes like this: When you're at work, you should be able to corral all your strong emotions, stop paying attention to them for eight or so hours, and concentrate on whatever it is you do to earn a living.

The workplace is a sacred space—sacred not in the spiritual sense but in the capitalistic sense. Check your emotional baggage at the door and put on your work hat. Especially in for-profit work environments, the workplace is for concentrating on tasks that grow the bottom line—and little else. Even in seemingly compassionate, human service-oriented businesses (I think of hospitals, daycare centers, nursing homes), the day-to-day processes and procedures allow little time for complex emotional and spiritual issues.

If you're in love, that's fine—but don't be using the workday to yearn for your soulmate. If you're upset about a financial problem at home, that's fine—but don't dwell on it from 8-5. And if you're sad over a loss in your life, we're sorry—but you're going to have to grin and bear it while you get the job done.

The truth is, we can't turn our emotions on and off like that. We're just not built that way. And to be healthy human beings, we need to pay attention to our emotions and give them expression—even during the workday.

In fact, I have this theory that our emotions are our souls talking to us. Our emotions and our "gut instincts" tell us whether we're doing the right thing or the wrong thing and whether we're living our lives in alignment with our values. When you feel joyous about something, it's probably something you're meant to do. When you feel uncomfortable about something, on the other hand, it's probably something you're not supposed to do. And when you feel sad about something? It's your soul telling you that it needs your time and loving attention.

Did you know that the word *courage* comes from the French word for heart (*coeur*)? Your courage grows for those things in life that impact you deeply. The death of someone you care about engages your heart; now you must muster the courage to mourn, even in the workplace.

And so when you feel strong feelings at work—whether they're strictly related to your work or not, I maintain that your feelings are telling you they need your immediate attention. When you're grieving and working at the same time and your grief feelings start to overpower everything else, you need to take a break and focus on your grief for a while. This book gives you many ideas for doing just that.

When a coworker dies

When someone in your workplace dies, you and your coworkers may struggle with the loss. The truth is, we often become closer to the people at work than we do to our own families. Why? One of the main reasons is that we spend so much more time with them. Think about how much time you spend talking to the person who sits next to you or down the hall from you at work. Now think about how much time you spend talking to your spouse or children. Measured in minutes, which is the more significant relationship in your day? (A sad but true reality...)

I hope you do care about the people you work with. A big part of my philosophy in this book is that the workplace cannot and should not be wholly separated from the rest of your life. If you seek and find no emotional and spiritual fulfillment in your job—which consumes so many of the precious hours of your life, you are doing yourself a disservice. This is not to say that your work needs to be like Mother Teresa's to count, but rather that connecting to others in your workplace makes for a richer life.

Of course, the double-edged sword of caring for someone else is that you will grieve when that person dies. To love is to one day mourn.

When a coworker dies and you and others are grieving, what do you do with your pain? First, you acknowledge it. Talk about it among yourselves. Attend the funeral—and participate in it if you can. Second, ask your company to help support you. A workplace grief support group led by a trained counselor may be helpful. And third, find ongoing ways to remember and pay tribute to the person who died.

This book contains a number of ideas for helping you mourn the death of a coworker. I hope you try some of them and that after a while, you share some of your ideas with me.

If you're not the griever

When someone is grieving, the entire workplace will no doubt be affected. That's how powerful grief is. If a coworker you care about has suffered the death of someone loved, that coworker's grief may be affecting you, too. Let's call it grief by association.

In grief by association, you may feel many of the same feelings as the griever. If the death was unexpected, you may be in shock. You certainly feel sad about the death. You may be angry that the death ever occurred. You feel powerless to help the person who's grieving. And you probably feel uncomfortable about how to deal with both your feelings and the feelings of the griever at work.

When you want to help someone who's grieving, the most important things you can do are 1) be there, and 2) listen. Being there means making yourself available as a friend. It means not avoiding the person who's grieving but instead going out of your way to visit with him, sit with him at lunch, and invite him to the social gathering that everybody else is going to on Friday.

I use the word *companion* to describe the kind of helper you can be to someone who is grieving. While you cannot take on his grief for him, you can be his companion now and then on the journey. You do not walk in front of or behind him; you walk beside him and seek to understand his experience.

Being a companion in grief also means being in it for the long haul. Especially at work, your impulse might be to tell the griever how sorry you are then act as if nothing happened. But grief isn't an event; it's an ongoing journey that the griever will experience for months, even years. You can help by keeping the conversation going with the person who's grieving. Ask her how she's doing when she comes back to work. Then ask her again the next week. And the next. And the next.

And when she answers, listen. Encourage her to talk about her thoughts and feelings. You don't need to have answers to her questions and you should be careful not to judge the thoughts and feelings she is expressing, but you can and should listen.

Now, you may be concerned about getting too involved in your coworker's personal life. If he wasn't your best buddy before the death, he doesn't need to be now, either. It's OK to set boundaries as you work to be a companion to him on his journey through grief. If you have 10 minutes to talk but no more, after 10 minutes have elapsed tell him you've got to get going but that you'd like to talk again later. Be helpful without getting more involved than feels comfortable to you. Keep in mind: You are not being a therapist, you are being a compassionate, supportive friend.

How to use this book

This book is for people who mourn and for people who want to help others who mourn. This book is for all those uncomfortable silences around the water cooler after a colleague has returned from a three-day bereavement leave. This book is for human resource managers and executives who've confronted the challenge of grief at work and want to do something positive about it.

And while this book targets the impact of death loss in the workplace, its principles and strategies apply to all the many forms that loss takes in our lives, such as divorce, job loss, financial troubles, serious illness, physical separation from those we love, etc. When something important to us is subtracted from our lives, whether it be our marriage, our health, our financial stability or any other defining characteristic, we grieve and mourn.

I compiled the 100 ideas in this book to help make grief at home in the workplace. Depending on your unique circumstances, you may be look-ing for something in particular in this book. You'll note that the first 20 ideas in the book are general principles about grief that everyone should understand. The next section (labeled For Mourners) is for you if you are currently grieving a death. The next section (labeled For Helpers) is for you if you need tips for supporting a coworker who is grieving. And the final section in this book, labeled In Traumatic Circumstances, are for workplaces affected by a tragedy such as a death that occurs in the workplace, a homicide, a suicide or an accident involving multiple employees.

Following this Introduction is a special message for executives, man-agers and human resource personnel. It addresses the organizational culture and policy issues that can create a compassionate workplace.

Attached to each of the 100 ideas is a *carpe diem*, which means "seize the day." Choose a carpe diem that seems like it might help you or someone else right this very moment and give it a try. Put your compassion into action and help create a work environment that embraces the normal and necessary process we call grief.

Alan D. Wolfelt

CREATING A CULTURE
OF COMPASSION

A special message for executives, managers and human resource personnel

I was recently honored to provide support to a woman whose 8-year-old daughter, Tia, died of a brain tumor. At home, the woman mourned in a variety of ways. At work, the woman simply displayed a single, precious photo of Tia on her desk.

On the one-year anniversary of the death, three of the woman's coworkers approached her. "It's been a year since Tia died," they noted. "We've talked about it and decided that you've had your year to mourn. Now it's time to put away the photo of Tia and move on."

This all-too-common workplace attitude is why I wrote this book. The story of Tia's mother is repeated across North America day after day. It's a hurtful story, an inhuman story and even, as I will explain, an unproductive story. It's high time to write a new narrative for grief in the workplace. For many reasons, it's time to re-establish a workplace culture that is more understanding, compassionate and supportive of grief.

Why our workplaces don't do grief

The Industrial Revolution of the late 19th and early 20th centuries brought speed, efficiency and profitability to the workplace. Like never before in the history of humankind, machinery and assembly line processes combined to boost productivity.

Where the horse-drawn carriage was made over the course of weeks and months by a single craftsman and his small team of apprentices, the new automobile was assembled in days in a large factory with hundreds of employees.

This new way of doing business made people more prosperous and it created goods that were affordable to the burgeoning middle class. As the Industrial Revolution unfolded, the average family could afford books, electricity, a telephone, mass-produced toys and clothing, a television and eventually a computer. Concurrent medical advances saved lives and doubled lifespans. As communication and travel technologies advanced, the whole world became accessible to everyone.

But we paid a price for this progress. The new business and community models traded intimacy for efficiency.

A hundred and fifty years ago, you and I probably would have worked in a small, family-run business in which we knew all our neighbors and patrons as well as we knew our own families. We would have lived in a community in which it was necessary to speak face-to-face to people (or write lengthy letters) to communicate with them.

When someone in our circle died, we would have understood in a profoundly personal way how the death affected everyone. Customs of the time would have demanded that we not only attended the lengthy visitation and funeral, but that we observed the mourning rituals for months after the death.

And while for practical reasons we may have been expected to return to work soon after the death, our grief would have been an understood backdrop to all our conversations and behaviors. The tempo of the workplace would have been much slower and more forgiving of our inability to concentrate. Our faith community, which would likely have been central to our daily lives, would have comforted us not only with their presence and their beliefs, but with practical help such as meals.

Grounded in the new business models of the Industrial Revolution, today's workplace all too often sees employees as machine-like and able to set aside emotions in order to be productive. Hogwash. Your gut tells you this isn't true. And as I'm about to demonstrate, so do the numbers.

Productivity and the grieving employee

In its annual "Grief Index" survey, the Grief Recovery Institute estimates that grief following the loss of a loved one costs America's businesses $37.5 billion dollars each year. Grief caused by divorce, family crisis and other types of loss add up to another $37 billion.

Grief in the workplace is expensive. Why? The main reason is that people who are grieving have a reduced ability to concentrate in the days, weeks, months, and sometimes even years after a death. Grief can feel like being in the middle of a wild, rushing river where you can't get a grasp on anything. Disconnected thoughts—some about the death, others about seemingly random topics—often race through the mourner's mind, making it hard to complete tasks. Powerful emotions well up repeatedly, overtaking the mind's capacity to think clearly and logically.

Seventy-five percent of mourners polled reported that their reduced ability to concentrate affected them in the workplace well beyond their allowed bereavement leave. And 50 percent said there were at least 30 work days following the death in which their lack of concentration significantly affected their work performance or even had negative repercussions. (And I'm sure these numbers are actually higher because people don't like to admit what is perceived as "weakness" or low performance, especially in the workplace.)

This reduced capacity to concentrate affects workers' ability to make good decisions, supervise others, and work safely.

- *Employees who can't concentrate tend to make bad decisions.* They may make costly mistakes, fail to act when they should, or act impulsively on incomplete information. And even when they make good decisions, they almost certainly take longer to do so.

- *Mourners in supervisory positions impact everyone they supervise.* When the supervisor makes a bad judgment, that judgment may be multiplied many times over as the repercussions ripple throughout the management chain.

- *Unsafe work behaviors may be the most visible and thus measurable result of the mourner's decreased capacity to concentrate.* Of the ten leading causes of workplace injuries resulting in workers missing five or more days of work (as reported by Liberty Mutual Insurance), seven are the direct result of a reduced ability to concentrate. These include falls, highway accidents, striking an object (e.g., walking into a doorframe), and getting caught in equipment. Fully 50 percent of blue collar workers affected by a death reported a higher incidence of injury in the days and weeks after the death.

I'm sure many of you have heard the term "presenteeism" to describe the negative consequences of workers coming to work when they aren't feeling well. Often cited causes of presenteeism are migraine headaches, allergies, asthma, arthritis, gastrointestinal disorders, and depression. Workers affected by these maladies cannot contribute 100 percent, so their productivity is affected. Some estimates posit that the phenomenon costs US companies more than $150 billion a year—much more than absenteeism, at $30 billion a year, does.

Grief at work is another form of presenteeism. The worker is there, struggling valiantly to work as expected, but his body and his mind and his spirit keep pushing his normal and necessary grief to the surface. So he's there but he's not there. The question is, how can we help him?

What's a workplace to do?

It is my contention that making the workplace more compassionate and grief-friendly is not only the right thing to do ethically, it's also the cost-saving approach. It's been proven that good preventive healthcare saves companies billions in healthcare costs. The same is likely true of proactive grief care.

The first step on the road to creating a grief-friendly work environment is to acknowledge that it's an issue. The second step is to put policies in place that support the grieving employee.

Your policy goal should be to create a culture of compassion. Much attention has been focused on the creation of quality-minded corporate cultures in the past two decades. Now what is needed is compassion reform.

The work-life theory of human resource management affirms that employees have lives into which work must fit (and not the other way around). Many of the work-life policies and initiatives are useful in establishing a culture of compassion in your organization.

As you read through the following suggestions, keep in mind that the costs of presenteeism are much greater than the costs of absenteeism, so the costs of effectively supporting the grieving employee will likely save you money in the long run.

- *Bereavement leave*—What's your company's bereavement leave policy? A typical bereavement leave allows three days off for the death of an immediate family member. If you've ever tried to plan a funeral, host a visitation, attend a funeral and see to out-of-town guests, not to mention travel if the death is not local, you know that three days paid leave isn't enough. A full work week's leave is much more realistic and enabling for the employee. Easily accessed unpaid leave is another option. Moreover, it's important that your bereavement leave policy allow for absences due to deaths outside the immediate family. The deaths of close friends, extended family members, neighbors, coworkers, gay partners and others can be as or more devastating than the death of an immediate family member.

- *Management practices*—How do your executives and managers respond when an employee is affected by a death? As with all aspects of corporate culture, management is responsible for modeling the desired behavior. Set up grief support training sessions for your management team. Help them roleplay empathetic responses. Establish clear standards for your company's bereavement management policies in your corporate documents.

- *Workplace counseling*—Your Employee Assistance Program should be able to help you set up individual counseling for mourners as well as a workplace grief group. If your business is too small to have a formal EAP program, you should seek out appropriate referral sources to provide support to your employees.

- *Workplace education*—Your employees need to be educated about your new culture of compassion. Just as you may have provided diversity training or CPR, you need to provide ongoing grief education. Employees need to learn about the normal and necessary process that is grief as well as your company's expectations about how to support coworkers who are grieving.

- *Stress relief*—In general, policies and culture shifts aimed at relieving stress in the workplace will be good for the grieving employee, too. Interior décor, lighting, background noise control, indoor air quality, and other environmental considerations can go a long way towards creating a comfortable, peaceful space in which to work—and grieve. Controlling work flow, offering the time and place to exercise, encouraging appropriate humor, and empowering employee decision-making are also fundamental grief support tools.

- *Flexibility*—Above all, when it comes to grief at work, encourage flexibility. Flexible bereavement leaves could be followed by flexible work schedules, alternative work arrangements, compressed work weeks, job sharing, telecommuting and other work-life program initiatives.

  For purposes of illustration, allow me to note that my own office manager at the Center for Loss is a bereaved parent. Her precious son, Mitch, died tragically several years ago. We have adjusted her work schedule to four days, Monday through Thursday, 8 am- 4 pm, to support her need for more time to attend to her grief and to renew herself. She participates in an ongoing support group (run by The Compassionate Friends) and talks openly in the workplace about her life-changing experience.

- *Creative programs*—Look into programs that other enlightened employers use to support grieving people and adapt them to your workplace. For example, Hallmark Cards has a program called Compassionate Connections, which is a volunteer employee support network. Employees who have faced a loss or personal challenge can sign up to support other employees struggling with the same issue.

The one-idea-per-page format of this book makes it an easy, quick read—something that mourners, with their reduced capacity to concentrate, need very much. I'd like to suggest that purchased in bulk, this book is affordable enough to make available to all your employees at times of need. It can also be used as a handbook for management training sessions.

I hope this book helps you establish a culture of compassion in your workplace, and I dream of the day when such a book won't be necessary because grief support at work will be so natural and intrinsic. In the meantime, thank you for your commitment to transforming North American business culture, one organization, one person, at a time.

1.

ACKNOWLEDGE THAT THE WORKPLACE IS A GRIEVING PLACE.

- As with all significant transitions in life, the death of someone loved affects every part of your being. In grief, you are impacted physically, emotionally, cognitively, socially, and spiritually.

- During your workday, you are not a different person than you are outside of work. Yes, you may be good at concentrating on your work skills while you're at work (just as you're good at concentrating on being a parent when you're at home or on being an athlete when you're playing a sport), but you're still a many-faceted person with a rich past, present, and future.

- After a death, your grief is an important part of who you are. And who you are is, of course, an important part of your job. You cannot separate your grief from your work.

- Because of the very nature of grief, the workplace is a grieving place. Just as the workplace is a place for celebrating birthdays, commiserating about parenting issues, and sharing opinions about virtually everything, it's a place for grieving—and, I hope, for supporting each other in grief.

CARPE DIEM

Understand that to "heal" in grief means to become whole again, to integrate your grief into your self and to learn to continue your changed life with fullness and meaning. The workplace is not only a grieving place, it can and should be a healing place.

2.

OVERCOME DESTRUCTIVE MISCONCEPTIONS ABOUT GRIEF AND MOURNING.

- You have probably internalized many of our society's harmful misconceptions about grief and mourning.

- Here are some to overcome:
  - Mourners need to be strong and carry on.
  - Tears are a sign of weakness.
  - People need to "get over" their grief.
  - The workplace isn't a place for sadness.
  - Death is something we don't talk about, especially at work.
  - If someone is grieving, the best thing to do is to leave him alone.
  - Time heals all wounds.
  - You can't help someone else with their grief.

- Sometimes these misconceptions will cause you to feel guilty about or ashamed of your true thoughts and feelings. Sometimes they cause you to back away from a friend in grief instead of reaching out to help.

- Grief is normal and necessary. Allow it to be what it is, and break through these misconceptions to help yourself as well as others in the workplace, at home, in your neighborhood—anywhere grief lives.

- For more on this topic, see the discussion of grief misconceptions at the end of this book.

CARPE DIEM
Which grief misconception do you identify with most strongly? Consider the ways in which you can help teach others about these destructive misconceptions.

3.

UNDERSTAND THE DIFFERENCE BETWEEN GRIEF AND MOURNING.

- Grief is the constellation of internal thoughts and feelings we have when someone loved dies. Grief is the container for our experience of loss. This container is stored within us.

- Mourning is the outward expression of grief. It's taking our feelings of grief and giving them expression outside of ourselves.

- Everyone grieves when someone loved dies, but if we are to integrate the loss into our lives, we must also mourn.

- Many of the ideas in this book are intended to help you mourn a death or help someone you care about mourn a death. Over time, and with the support of others, to mourn is to heal.

- It is appropriate to mourn during the workday, for to not mourn is to sell out your soul. When you feel the need to, sporadically and in small doses, you should. This book will give you some ideas that will help you mourn effectively at work or support someone else who is mourning at work.

CARPE DIEM
Ask yourself this: In my life, have I not only grieved, but also mourned? How so?

4.

BELIEVE IN THE POWER OF STORY.

- A vital part of healing in grief is often "telling the story."

- When people are in mourning, they often feel the need to tell the story of the life and the death to others. It helps them acknowledge the reality of the death and begin the transition from life before the death to life after the death.

- At work, telling the story allows coworkers to be part of the story, too. In order to be supportive, everyone needs to know what has happened. But remember that not everyone will be able to be a compassionate listener. End-of-life stories are difficult to hear.

- Not all mourners want to talk about the death. Preferring privacy is OK, too, as long as the mourner isn't shutting others out altogether. Keeping thoughts and feelings about the death inside only makes them more powerful. Giving them voice allows some control over them.

- If you're supporting someone who's in mourning, respect the power of story. If the mourner wants to tell her story, listen without judgment. If she tends to repeat her story, try to be a patient and ongoing source of support.

CARPE DIEM

Today, make it a point to be a grief storyteller or a story-listener at work. Respect workplace boundaries while still opening up and sharing your life with someone you care about.

5.

RECOGNIZE THE EMOTIONS OF GRIEF.

- People in grief often experience a wide range of emotions.

- Some of the most common emotions in grief include:
  - shock and numbness
  - disorganization and confusion
  - anxiety and fear
  - explosive emotions, such as anger, blame and resentment
  - guilt and regret
  - sadness
  - relief and release

- As strange as some of these emotions may seem, they are common and they are true. They are what they are. No emotion is right or wrong, and all are deserving of attention and respect.

CARPE DIEM

Empathy is the art of entering into the emotional world of another person. Become a more empathetic person today by truly listening to someone else and making an effort to understand and feel compassion towards him.

6.

RECOGNIZE THE PHYSICAL SYMPTOMS OF GRIEF.

- When people are in grief, their bodies often take on some of the stress of the experience.

- This stress can lead to common bodily symptoms, such as:
  - troubles with sleeping
  - low energy
  - muscle aches and pains
  - shortness of breath
  - tightness in the throat or chest
  - digestive problems
  - heart palpitations
  - nausea
  - headaches
  - changes in appetite
  - weight loss or gain

- The "lethargy of grief" often causes mourners to feel exhausted and chronically low in energy.

- In addition, pre-existing or chronic health problems can become more pronounced during times of grief.

CARPE DIEM

Taking care of your body during times of stress is a good, proactive approach to helping yourself cope. Today, model healthy eating and exercise habits at work.

7.

RECOGNIZE THE COGNITIVE EFFECTS OF GRIEF.

- Grief affects our ability to think, absorb information, make decisions and reason logically.

- Often, grief causes the mourners' minds to return to the circumstances of the death and the surreal reality of the death over and over again. At times it's as if they can't stop thinking about the loss.

- Even when they're not consciously thinking about the death, their subconscious minds can be absorbed with trying to acknowledge the new reality of life without the person who died.

- Mourners often struggle with short-term memory problems and have trouble making decisions. They also may seem confused and unable to pay attention.

- Cognitive difficulties such as these are normal and temporary. As time passes and as the mourner's grief needs are met, cognitive deficits will slowly reverse.

CARPE DIEM

Help someone who is mourning by putting it in writing. If the mourner is expected to complete a task, write down all the details for her.

8.

RECOGNIZE THE SOCIAL REPERCUSSIONS OF GRIEF.

- Grief is hard on everyone. It's not only hard on the mourner, but it can also be very hard on the mourner's family, friends, coworkers, neighbors, etc. because supporting others in grief is draining.

- When someone in your workplace is grieving, you may assume that his family and close friends are meeting his emotional needs. This often isn't true. Family and friends often avoid or abandon mourners because they are uncomfortable being in the presence of the painful process of grief.

- Many times friends and family don't know how to support the mourner so they instead do nothing. The worst thing you can do is nothing. Don't worry so much about what you should say or how you should say it. Just listen and be available.

- Some mourners isolate themselves in a misguided attempt to cope with their grief. It's true that a certain amount of withdrawal can be necessary to deal with the spiritual challenges of grief, but when the mourner over-isolates, he cuts off the very lifelines of social and emotional support that can save him.

CARPE DIEM
Stick together. Reach out to someone at work who needs your social support right now.

9.

RECOGNIZE THE SPIRITUAL NATURE OF GRIEF.

- At its most fundamental, grief is a spiritual journey. It results in the "dark night of the soul"—a profoundly defining period in which the mourner must wrestle with his beliefs about life and death.

- Why go on living? Why do people have to die? Why do we have to suffer so? What is the purpose of my life? Is there really a God and an afterlife? Will I see the person who died again? These are the sorts of questions that often consume the mourner's heart and soul.

- The mourner's work life may also be called into question. Am I doing the job I'm meant to do? Is my work meaningful? This sort of vocational questioning is normal and necessary. The more supported the mourner is at work, however, the more likely she will be to find continued meaning in her work life.

CARPE DIEM

Spend a few minutes jotting down your thoughts about what makes your work meaningful. How can you make it more meaningful?

10.

BE ON THE LOOKOUT FOR DISENFRANCHISED GRIEF.

- When a person experiences a death that is not openly acknowledged, publicly mourned and/or socially accepted, we say that her grief is "disenfranchised."

- Deaths from AIDS, suicide, and homicide often result in the disenfranchised grief of family and friends because society as a whole doesn't "accept" these deaths as readily.

- In the workplace, you might notice that some types of deaths are supported more easily than others. The death of a child, for example, might be acknowledged more openly than the death of a lover or an older parent.

- Remember that a mourner's grief is usually as strong as the mourner's attachment was to the person who died. This means that the grief following the death of a friend (or even a pet) can be as strong or stronger than the death of a family member, for example.

- All mourners need our support. Don't assume that certain types of losses are less painful or less meaningful than others. Don't let any sort of grief be disenfranchised in your workplace.

CARPE DIEM

Think for a few moments about who in your workplace might be suffering from disenfranchised grief. Today, make it a point to sit and visit with this person for a few minutes.

11.

UNDERSTAND THE SIX NEEDS OF MOURNING

Need #1: Acknowledge the reality of the death.

- Mourners must gently confront the difficult reality that someone they loved is dead and will never physically be present to them again.

- Whether the death was sudden or anticipated, acknowledging the full reality of the loss may occur over weeks and months.

- If you are in grief, you will first acknowledge the reality of the loss with your head. Only over time will you come to acknowledge it with your heart. As Stephen Levine has noted, "There are pains that cannot be contained in the mind, only in the heart."

- At times mourners push away the reality of the death. This is normal. They come to integrate the reality in doses as they are ready.

CARPE DIEM

If you are grieving, tell someone about the death today. Talking about it will help you work on this important need.

12.

UNDERSTAND THE SIX NEEDS OF MOURNING

Need #2: Embrace the pain of the loss.

• This need requires mourners to embrace the pain of their loss—something we naturally don't want to do. It is easier to avoid, repress or push away the pain of grief than it is to confront it.

• It is in embracing your grief, however, that you will learn to reconcile yourself to it.

• Mourners need to slowly—ever so slowly—"dose" themselves in embracing their pain. If they were to allow in all the pain at once, they could not survive.

• People with chronic pain are taught not to tighten around the pain but to relax and allow the pain to be present. When pain is resisted, it intensifies. You don't want to fight with your pain; you want to allow it into your soul in small doses so that eventually you can move from darkness into light.

CARPE DIEM

Think about a time you confronted or embraced something painful in your life rather than choosing to ignore it. How did you feel afterward?

13.

UNDERSTAND THE SIX NEEDS OF MOURNING

Need #3: Remember the person who died.

- When someone loved dies, they live on in us through memory.

- To heal, mourners need to actively remember the person who died and commemorate the life that was lived.

- If you are grieving, never let anyone take your memories away in a misguided attempt to save you from pain. It's good for you to continue to display photos of the person who died. It's good to think about your memories and share them with others.

- Remembering the past makes hoping for the future possible. As Kierkegaard noted, "While life must eventually be lived forward, it can only be understood backward."

CARPE DIEM

If you are grieving, brainstorm a list of characteristics or memories of the person who died. Write as fast as you can for 10 minutes (or more), then put away your list for later reflection.

14.

UNDERSTAND THE SIX NEEDS OF MOURNING

Need #4: Develop a new self-identity.

- Part of your self-identity is formed by the relationships you have with other people in your life. I am not just Alan Wolfelt; I am also a son, a husband, a father, a friend.

- When someone you care about dies, your self-identity is changed. You may go from being a "wife" to a "widow" or from a "parent" to a "bereaved parent." The way you defined yourself and the way society defines you is changed.

- Mourners need to re-anchor themselves, to reconstruct their self-identities. This is arduous and painful work. One of their biggest challenges may be to recreate themselves in the face of the loss of who they once were.

- Many mourners discover that as they work on this need, they ultimately discover some positive changes, such as becoming more caring or less judgmental.

CARPE DIEM
Make a list of all the various aspects of your self that make up your self-identity.

15.

UNDERSTAND THE SIX
NEEDS OF MOURNING

Need #5: Search for meaning.

- When someone loved dies, we naturally question the meaning and purpose of life and death.

- "Why?" questions may surface uncontrollably and often precede "How" questions. "Why did this happen?" comes before "How will I go on living?"

- Mourners question their philosophies of life and explore religious and spiritual values as they work on this need.

- Remember that having faith or spirituality does not negate the need to mourn. "Blessed are those who mourn for they shall be comforted."

CARPE DIEM

Talk to someone at work about their faith or spirituality.
Find out what gives them peace.

16.

UNDERSTAND THE SIX NEEDS OF MOURNING

Need #6: Receive ongoing support from others.

• As mourners, we need the love and understanding of others if we are to integrate the loss into our lives.

• Unfortunately, our society places too much value on "carrying on" and "doing well" after a death. So, many mourners are abandoned by their friends and family—and coworkers—soon after the death.

• One of the touchstones of grief is that each and every one of us as humans are connected by loss. As you experience the physical separation from someone you love, you are connected to every single person who has experienced or ever will experience a similar loss. As The Compassionate Friends (an international organization of bereaved parents) say, "We need not walk alone."

• If you are grieving, don't feel ashamed by your dependence on others right now. Instead, revel in the knowledge that others care about you.

• Grief is a process, not an event, and mourners need the continued support of friends and family for weeks, months and years.

CARPE DIEM
Offer support today to someone in your workplace who needs it.

17.

KNOW THAT GRIEF DOES NOT PROCEED IN ORDERLY, PREDICTABLE "STAGES."

- Though the "Needs of Mourning" (Ideas 11-16) are numbered 1-6, grief is not an orderly progression towards reconciliation. Don't fall into the trap of thinking that grief is predictable or always forward-moving.

- Usually, grief hurts more before it hurts less.

- I once heard grief compared to Alice's fall into the rabbit hole. One moment Alice is dozing in the garden and the next she is falling into a world where nothing is right. Who is she? Where is she going? Why does nothing make sense? Slowly, over time and after many tribulations, Alice wakes up. But she will never look at things as she did before.

- Mourners often experience a multitude of different emotions in a wave-like fashion. They also typically encounter more than one need of mourning at the same time.

CARPE DIEM
Have you heard people explain the "stages" of grief? The theory of stages was originally interpreted from the experiences of the dying. Grief is rarely so neat. Don't allow yourself or anyone else to compartmentalize your grief.

18.

UNDERSTAND THE CONCEPT OF RECONCILIATION.

- Sometimes you'll hear about "recovering" from grief. This term is damaging because it implies that grief is an illness that must be cured. It also connotes a return to the way things were before the death.

- We don't recover from grief. We become "reconciled" to it. In other words, we learn to live with it and are forever changed by it.

- This does not mean a life of misery, however. We often not only heal but grow through grief. Of course we are never glad that the person has died, but our lives can potentially be deeper and more meaningful after a death.

- Reconciliation takes time. Sometimes mourners do not become truly reconciled to their loss for years and even then have "grief-bursts" (see Idea 44) forever.

- If you are grieving, you will recognize that you are reconciling your grief when you again have the capacity to enjoy life and plan for the future. Your eating and sleeping habits will have stabilized. You will find yourself loving and being loved—nurturing your relationships with others. You will feel aware that while you will never "get over" your grief, your life does have a new reality, meaning and purpose.

CARPE DIEM

Think about the past losses in your life and the ways in which you've learned to reconcile yourself to them.

19.

KNOW THAT YOUR WORKPLACE IS FOREVER CHANGED.

- Grief changes us. Who we were before a death is different from who we are after a death.

- After death touches your workplace, it will never be quite the same as it was before. If a coworker has died, you will always feel his absence. If a coworker's family member dies, the death becomes part of the fabric of the workplace.

- The changes death brings to the workplace are usually subtle. Unless your workplace was touched by a major tragedy, you will probably not feel a significant difference after a death. But you will know in your heart of hearts that each death that impacts your workplace leaves an indelible mark.

- Just as we incorporate new babies and new friends and new colleagues into our lives, we incorporate their absence when they leave us. This give and take is what, in many ways, defines our lives.

CARPE DIEM

Think about people you've worked with in the past but who are no longer a part of your current life. How did these people affect who you are today?

20.

LOOK FOR GROWTH IN GRIEF.

- Over time, mourners often find that they are growing emotionally and spiritually as a result of their grief. Though they would often gladly trade this growth for one more minute with the person who died, death brings bittersweet gifts into their lives that they would not otherwise have.

- Many people emerge from their early grief as stronger, more capable people. They may be more assertive and apt to say what they really believe. They've learned what's truly important and what's not.

- Never force growth on a mourner before she's ready. It's inappropriate to say, "You'll grow because of this" or "This will make you a better person." You can be a witness to her growth as it unfolds, but foretelling her growth only discounts her here-and-now pain.

CARPE DIEM
Have you grown through grief during your life?
Consider the ways in which this may be so.

WHEN SOMEONE YOU
CARE ABOUT DIES

Someone you care about has died. You are in mourning. You are
bereft. To be "bereaved" literally means "to be torn apart" and "to
have special needs." I am truly sorry for your loss.

Perhaps your most important special need right now is to be compassionate with yourself. The word compassion means "with passion." So,
self-compassion means caring for oneself "with passion." Be kind to
yourself. Over my years of walking with people in grief, I have discov-
ered that many of us are hard on ourselves when we are in mourning.
We have inappropriate expectations of how "well" we should be doing
with our grief.

These expectations result from common societal messages that tell us
to be strong in the face of grief. We are told to "carry on," to "keep
your chin up," and to "keep busy." Actually, when we are in grief we
need to slow down, to turn inward, to embrace our feelings of loss
and to seek and accept support.

Care for yourself with passion. For it is in nurturing ourselves, in
allowing ourselves the time and the loving attention we need to journey through our grief, that we find meaning in our continued living.

21.

ALLOW FOR NUMBNESS.

- Feelings of shock, numbness and disbelief are nature's way of temporarily protecting us from the full reality of a death. They help us survive our early grief.

- We often think, "I will wake up and this will not have happened." Grief can feel like being in a dream.

- It's very hard to feel numb and in shock and try to concentrate on work at the same time. You really can't do it and if you try, you're probably not going to be very effective at your job. In certain kinds of jobs, your inability to concentrate may even be dangerous.

- If you're feeling intense psychic numbing because of the death of someone you care about, take time off work if at all possible. If your company allows only inadequate bereavement leave, talk to your supervisor or human resources manager about taking vacation time, a family leave of absence, or an unpaid leave.

- IF POSSIBLE, don't come back to work until the acute aftershock wears off. You may well still feel somewhat numb weeks later, and you won't be fully functioning yet, but the intense numbness will have faded.

CARPE DIEM

If you're feeling numb, cancel any commitments that require concentration and decision-making. Allow yourself time to regroup.

22.

BE COMPASSIONATE WITH YOURSELF.

- The journey through grief is a long and difficult one. It is also a journey for which there is no preparation.

- Be compassionate with yourself as you encounter painful thoughts and feelings. Do what you have to do to survive the coming weeks and months.

- Don't judge yourself or try to set a particular course for healing. You are NOT going crazy and there is no one right way to do this.

- When you were a child your parents probably told you that if you got lost, you should stay put. Don't go anywhere. Wait. Wait and call out for help.

- Let your grief journey be what it is. And let yourself—your new, grieving self—be who you are.

CARPE DIEM
Share some quiet time with someone wonderful in your life.
Let that person know how important he is to you.

23.

TAKE GOOD CARE OF YOURSELF.

- Good self-care is nurturing and necessary for mourners, yet it's something many of us completely overlook.

- Try very hard to eat well. At work it can be tempting to not eat at all or to succumb to workplace junk food. But keep in mind that you're asking a lot of your body right now. You're asking it to grieve and work at the same time (not to mention all the other demands on your life). If you don't fuel it well, your body won't keep up.

- Get adequate rest. Even if you're not sleepy, lay your body down 2-3 times a day for 20 minutes. Listen to what your body tells you. "Get some rest," it says. "But I don't have time," you reply. "I have things to do." "OK, then, I'll get sick so you HAVE to rest," your body says. And it will get sick if that's what it takes to get its needs met!

- Drink at least 5-6 glasses of water each day. Dehydration can compound feelings of fatigue and disorientation. Every morning at work, fill a quart container with water and make it a goal to drink it up by the day's end.

- Exercise not only provides you with more energy, it can give you focused thinking time. Take a 20-minute break from work to walk every day. Or, if that seems too much, a five-minute walk. But don't over-exercise, because your body needs extra rest, as well.

- Now more than ever, you need to allow time for you.

CARPE DIEM
Are you taking a multi-vitamin? If not,
now is probably a good time to start.

24.

REACH OUT TO OTHERS FOR HELP.

- Perhaps the most compassionate thing you can do for yourself at this difficult time is to reach out to others for help.

- Think of it this way: Grieving may be the hardest work you have ever done. And hard work is less burdensome when others lend a hand. Life's greatest challenges—getting through school, raising children, pursuing a career—are in many ways team efforts. So it should be with mourning.

- Sharing your pain with others won't make it disappear, but it will, over time, make it more bearable.

- Reaching out for help also connects you to other people and strengthens the bonds of love that make life seem worth living again.

- Reaching out for support at work will make your work life a more integral part of your grief journey. It will make your time at work a more honest and whole reflection of who you are right now. It will also help you heal.

CARPE DIEM

Don't expect that everyone in your life will be able to support you in your grief. I use the rule of thirds: typically one-third will turn out to be truly empathic helpers; one-third will be neutral; and one-third will be harmful to you in your efforts to mourn and heal.

25.

IDENTIFY THREE PEOPLE AT WORK YOU CAN TURN TO ANYTIME YOU NEED A FRIEND.

- You may have many people who care about you but few who are able to be good companions in grief.

- Identify three people in your workplace whom you think can be there for you in the coming weeks and months.

- Don't assume that others will help. Even normally compassionate people sometimes find it hard to be present to others in grief.

- When you're feeling your grief during the workday, reach out to one of your three grief companions. Ask her if she could have lunch with you or stop by her desk to chat for a few minutes.

- Don't restrain yourself from reaching out for help; often your coworkers want to help but don't know how. Talking to you about your thoughts and feelings is one of the best ways they can help, and if you initiate the conversation, they're often ready and willing to listen.

CARPE DIEM
Who are your three potential grief companions at work?
Mull this over today.

26.

KEEP A JOURNAL.

- Journals are an ideal way for some mourners to record thoughts and feeling.

- Remember—your inner thoughts and feelings of grief need to be expressed outwardly (which includes writing) if you are to integrate this death into your life.

- Don't worry about what you're writing or how well you're writing it. Just write whatever comes into your mind. To get started, set a timer for five or ten minutes and write as much as you can without stopping.

- At work, journal writing is a way to mourn without disrupting the workplace. When you feel your grief demanding your attention, stay at your desk, open your journal, and spend a few minutes writing. (Or you can keep a journal on your computer, if you'd prefer.) Write about whatever's on your mind at the moment. Pour out your thoughts and feelings onto the page. After you've written as much as you feel the need to, tuck the journal back into a drawer, take a deep breath, and decide if you're ready to concentrate on your work.

CARPE DIEM

Stop by your local bookstore and choose a blank book you like the look and feel of. Bring it to work and spend a few minutes writing your first entry. If you want a more structured journal, which asks questions then provides space for answers, take a look at my *Understanding Your Grief Journal* at bookstores or www.centerforloss.com.

27.

BE PROACTIVE IN YOUR JOURNEY THROUGH GRIEF.

- Our society teaches us that emotional pain is to be avoided, not embraced, yet it is only in moving toward our grief that we can be healed.

- As Helen Keller once said, "The only way to the other side is through." Be sure to open the door slowly and only when you are ready. Keep in mind that there are no rewards for speed!

- Being proactive in grief means taking an active role in your healing. Empower yourself to "do something" with your grief—to mourn it, to express it outside yourself, to find ways to help yourself heal.

- Be suspicious if you find yourself thinking that you're "doing well" since the death. Sometimes "doing well" means you're avoiding your pain.

CARPE DIEM

Today, do something to confront and express your grief. Maybe it's time to tell someone close to you how you've really been feeling.

28.

DON'T EXPECT TO MOURN
OR HEAL IN A CERTAIN
AMOUNT OF TIME.

- There is no set timetable for grief. It never really ends, and the journey to reconciliation (see Idea 18) lasts as long as it lasts. Don't expect to be "over" your grief in a certain number of months or even years.

- Time is almost irrelevant when it comes to grief. You've heard it said that time heals all wounds. While grief does tend to soften over the years, healing has more to do with the six needs of mourning being met than with time itself.

- At work, help your supervisor and coworkers understand that you don't know how long you'll be feeling intense grief and that establishing any kind of "deadline" is inappropriate.

CARPE DIEM

Talk to your supervisor about your need to survive day by
day for now and avoid planning long-term.

29.

EMBRACE THE UNIQUENESS OF YOUR GRIEF.

- Your grief is what it is. The thoughts and feelings you've been having since the death are what they are. They are neither good nor bad, right nor wrong. They simply are.

- Your unique grief journey will be shaped by many factors, including:
  - the nature of the relationship you had with the person who died.
  - the age of the person who died.
  - the circumstances of the death.
  - your unique personality.
  - your cultural background.
  - your religious or spiritual beliefs.
  - your gender.
  - your support systems.

- Your grief is unique. There is only one you. And your relationship with the person who died was unique. The circumstances of the death make it unique, too. Go slow.

- Just as you must accept the uniqueness of your own grief, you must also accept the grief responses of others. Others who loved the person who died will grieve in very different ways. Accept these differences and do not judge others for their unique thoughts and feelings.

CARPE DIEM

Today, talk to someone else grieving this death. Share your thoughts and feelings. You may be surprised at both the differences and the similarities.

30.

CRY.

- Tears are a natural cleansing and healing mechanism. They rid your body of stress chemicals. It's OK to cry. In fact, it's good to cry when you feel like it. What's more, tears are a form of mourning. They are sacred!

- Your pain, your grief, your overwhelming loss disturbs the world around you. Disturb the quiet with your soul's cry.

- On the other hand, don't feel bad if you aren't crying a lot. Not everyone is a crier.

- You may find that those around you are uncomfortable with your tears. As a society, we're often not so good at witnessing others in pain. Don't let those people take your grief away from you.

- Explain to your friends and family that you need to cry right now and that they can help by allowing you to.

- You may find yourself crying at unexpected times or places. If you're at work and you need to cry, excuse yourself and retreat to somewhere private.

CARPE DIEM

If you feel like it, have a good cry today. Find a safe place to embrace your pain and cry as long and as hard as you want to.

31.

EMBRACE YOUR SPIRITUALITY.

- Above all, grief is a journey of the soul. It demands you to consider why people live, why people die and what gives life meaning. These are the most spiritual questions we have language to form.

- Your workplace doesn't need to be devoid of spirituality. You might hang a small spiritual symbol in your cubicle or bring a religious text to read over your lunch break. If others share your faith, you might ask them to gather with you over lunchtime once a week or once a month to discuss religious texts or spiritual ideas.

- You may want to find books in which other people have shared their struggles with spirituality after a death. From a Christian perspective, some of my favorites are *A Grace Disguised*, by Gerald L. Sittser; *A Grief Observed*, by C.S. Lewis; and *The Will of God*, by Leslie Weatherhead. Also popular is *When Bad Things Happen to Good People*, by Rabbi Harold Kushner.

- Make the effort to embrace your spirituality and it will embrace you back by inspiring you with a sense of peace, hope and healing.

CARPE DIEM

Perhaps you have a friend who seems spiritually grounded. Talk to this person about his beliefs and spiritual experiences. Ask him how he learned to nurture his spirituality.

32.

THINK OF YOUR GRIEF
AS PART OF YOUR WORK.

- You probably take your work very seriously. You know you need to be on time and complete the tasks expected of you. You care about doing your job well and thoroughly. And you also know that there are serious repercussions if you fail to meet expectations at work.

- Your grief is work, too—maybe the hardest work you have ever done, and you need to take it seriously, as well. It demands your time and your attention, today and in the weeks and months to come.

- If you don't do your grief work (by expressing your grief outside yourself in authentic and ongoing ways), there are also serious repercussions. You may become physically ill. You may become emotionally "stuck." And you may well feel spiritually empty for the rest of your life.

- If you want to live and love fully again, you need to do your grief work.

CARPE DIEM

Schedule some grief time into your work calendar. Make an appointment with yourself to write in your journal, visit the cemetery or scattering site, or attend a support group.

33.

STAY IN TOUCH WITH YOUR FEELINGS.

- You will probably feel many different feelings in the coming weeks and months. You may feel, among other things, numb, angry, guilty, afraid, confused and, of course, deeply sad. Sometimes these feelings will follow each other within a short period of time or they may occur simultaneously.

- As strange as some of these emotions may seem to you, they are normal. Your feelings are what they are. They are not right or wrong, they simply are. Allow yourself to feel whatever it is you are feeling without judging yourself.

- Stay in touch with your feelings by leaning into them when you are ready. If you feel angry, for example, allow yourself to feel and think through this anger. Don't suppress it or distract yourself from it. Instead, acknowledge your feelings and give them voice. At work, tell a friend, "I feel so mad today because ..." or write in your journal, "I feel such regret that..."

CARPE DIEM

How are you feeling about the death right now, right this minute?
Name your feelings and write about them for a few minutes.

34.

DON'T TAKE ON ADDITIONAL STRESSES RIGHT NOW.

- Your plate is full right now—physically, emotionally, cognitively, socially and spiritually. Now is *not* the time to take on additional stress in the form of increased workload, new commitments,   elective life changes, etc.

- If you can (and I realize this isn't always possible), try to avoid making any major decisions for at least a year following the death. Life changes such as moving to a new house or a new city, switching jobs, or getting divorced or remarried may seem like proactive, positive steps. But often such major upheavals only compound stress and delay your mourning.

- At work, one of the best ways to be compassionate with yourself right now is to say no. No, I can't take on that task. No, I'm sorry, but I wouldn't be very effective at that. No, I simply can't. If you've always been a willing and capable worker in the past, your employer will understand your temporary need to lighten your load.

- Keep your life simple right now. Do what you need to do to get through the day. Spend your time with people you love, doing the things that give you pleasure. Eliminate or set limits with friends who drain you or make you feel worse when you're around them.

CARPE DIEM
Talk to your supervisor about easing your workload for the time-being.

35.

SPEND TIME ALONE.

- Reaching out to others while we're in mourning is necessary. Mourning is hard work and we can't get through it by ourselves.

- Still, you will also need alone time to gently work on the six needs of mourning. To slow down and to turn inward, you must sometimes insist on solitude.

- As the famous Swiss psychiatrist Carl Jung wrote, "When you are up against a wall, be still and put down roots, until clarity comes from deeper sources to see over the wall."

- At work, you may sometimes feel the need to be alone with your grief. Depending on your work environment, that may be difficult. Try stepping outside for a short walk, or go sit in your car for a few minutes.

- Don't shut your coworkers, friends and family out altogether, but do heed the call for contemplative silence.

CARPE DIEM
Schedule one hour of solitude into your day today.

36.

SURROUND YOURSELF
WITH MEMORIES.

- As I have shared, one of the needs that all mourners have is to remember those who have died.

- You can remember while you're at work, too. If you are actively grieving, make sure to display at least one photo of the person who died.

- It might seem counterintuitive to keep this photo at work; after all, won't it just make you sad? Yes, it may make you feel a little sad, but it will also help you direct your grief feelings throughout the workday. And as you know, you are already sad.

- When your grief calls to you during the workday, try focusing on the photo of the person who died. Remember his smile. Remember the day the photo was taken. Remember why you loved him so much.

- Other ways to surround yourself with memories at work include keeping a linking object at your desk (see Idea 37) and listening to music that reminds you of the person who died.

CARPE DIEM
Thoughtfully frame a special photo or collection of
photos and bring them to work this week.

37.

UNDERSTAND THE ROLE OF LINKING OBJECTS.

- You may be comforted by physical objects associated with the person who died. You may save clothing, jewelry, toys, locks of hair and other personal items.

- Such "linking objects" may help you remember the person who died and honor the life that was lived. Such objects may help you heal.

- Never think that being attached to these objects is morbid or wrong.

- Never hurry into disposing of the personal effects of the person who died. You may want to leave personal items untouched for months or sometimes years. This is OK as long as the objects offer comfort and don't inhibit healing.

- Watch out for people who try to tell you that if you force yourself to get rid of linking objects, it will help you "accept" the loss. These people may be well-intentioned but are sadly misinformed.

CARPE DIEM

When and only when you're ready, ask a friend or family member to help you sort through the personal belongings of the person who died. Fill a memory box with significant objects and mementos.

38.

LIGHT A CANDLE.

- Throughout history, cultures have lit candles as part of ceremonies. There is something about the act of lighting a candle (and extinguishing it) that is both symbolic and sacred. Watching the flickering candle is often part of the ceremony, too.

- If your workplace allows it (and it's a safe environment in which to do so), keep a candle at your desk to light to acknowledge your grief. Light the candle, focus on the flame, and spend a few minutes breathing deeply. Allow yourself to experience your grief while at the same time aligning yourself with your intention to heal. Don't forget to blow out the candle when you're finished.

- Lighting an aromatherapy candle adds the additional healing benefits of smell. Our sense of smell is tied in powerful ways to our memories and to various centers in the brain. Choose a scent that makes you feel hopeful and centered.

CARPE DIEM
Buy a small candle you like in a safe, glass container to keep at work.

39.

IGNORE HURTFUL ADVICE.

- Sometimes well-intentioned but misinformed friends (who are often in the one-third of people who are destructive to your grief) will hurt you unknowingly with their words.

- You may be told:
  - I know how you feel.
  - Get on with your life.
  - Keep your chin up.
  - It was God's will.
  - Be glad it was quick.
  - Think of all you have to be thankful for.
  - Now you have an angel in heaven.
  - Time heals all wounds.
  - You're strong. You'll get through this.

- Don't take this advice to heart. Such clichés are often offered because people don't know what else to say. The problem is, phrases like these diminish your unique and significant loss.

CARPE DIEM

Before your loss, did you ever offer some of these very same phrases to others touched by grief? Most of us have. Learn to forgive these all-too-human mistakes.

40.

GET HELP WITH
FINANCIAL STRESSES.

- Death often causes financial difficulties on top of the emotional and spiritual stresses. Emergency medical care can be very expensive. Lost work time, attorney's fees, and travel costs can all contribute to financial overload.

- If you or your family is under financial stress right now, ask for help. Ask someone you trust to take charge of your finances right now so you can concentrate on your grief. Call your consumer credit counseling agency. Consolidate your debts with a home equity loan.

- At work, your human resources department may help you with medical insurance claims, life insurance policies, access to your 401K savings, and other financial issues. If you need financial help of any kind, make an appointment with a human resources manager today.

- Whatever you do, don't ignore your finances right now. Delinquencies and defaulting on loans will only cause you bigger headaches in the months to come.

CARPE DIEM
Make an appointment to sit down with a qualified,
non-commissioned financial or human resources expert
and review your short-term finances.

41.

REACH OUT AND TOUCH.

- For many people, physical contact with another human being is healing. It has been recognized since ancient times as having transformative, healing powers.

- Have you hugged anyone lately? Held someone's hand? Put your arm around another human being?

- You probably know several people who enjoy hugging or physical touching. If you're comfortable with their touch, encourage it in the weeks and months to come.

- Hug someone you feel safe with. Kiss your children or a friend's baby. Walk arm in arm with a neighbor.

- At work, it's sometimes appropriate to touch others. A hug or even a touch on the arm can help you make it through the day.

CARPE DIEM
Schedule an appointment today for a massage
with a trained massage therapist.

42.

WRITE A LETTER.

- Sometimes articulating our thoughts and feelings in letter-form helps us understand them better.

- Write a letter to the person who died telling her how you feel now that she's gone. Consider the following prompts:
  - What I miss most about you is . . .
  - What I wish I'd said or hadn't said is . . .
  - What's hardest for me now is . . .
  - What I'd like to ask you is . . .
  - I'm keeping my memories of you alive by . . .

- Read your letter aloud at the cemetery or any other sacred place you think appropriate.

- Another healing exercise can be writing a letter to yourself on behalf of the person who died. Imagine that the person who died is writing you from heaven. What would she say to you? How would she want you to live the rest of your life?

- Write a letter to God telling him how you feel about the death.

- Write thank you notes to helpers such as hospice staff, neighbors, doctors, funeral directors, etc.

CARPE DIEM
Write a letter to someone who's still alive telling her
why she's so important to you.

43.

SEEK SUPPORT ON ANNIVERSARIES.

- Anniversaries—of the death, life events, birthdays—can be especially hard when you are in grief.

- These are times you may want to plan ahead for. The anniversary of the death may be a good day to plan a small memorial service at the site of the death or the cemetery or scattering site. Ritualizing your thoughts and feelings through prayer, song and memory-sharing with others will help create positive, healing structure on this day.

- Reach out to others on birthdays and other anniversaries. Talk about your feelings with a close friend.

CARPE DIEM

What's the next anniversary you've been anticipating?
Make a plan right now for what you will do on that day.
Enlist a friend's help so you won't be alone.

44.

DON'T BE CAUGHT OFF GUARD BY "GRIEFBURSTS."

- Sometimes heightened periods of sadness may overwhelm you. These times can seem to come of out nowhere and can be frightening and painful.

- Even long after the death, something as simple as a sound, a smell or a phrase can bring on a "griefburst." You may see someone in a crowd who resembles the person who died. You may come across an old jacket or tennis racquet that belonged to the person who died. You may smell a certain food or cologne that reminds you of the person who died. These experiences tend to trigger sudden, unexpected and powerful waves of emotion.

- I often think that griefbursts are the way the person who has died says to you, "Don't forget me. Please don't forget me."

- Allow yourself to experience griefbursts without shame or self-judgment, no matter where and when they occur. If you would feel more comfortable, retreat to somewhere private when these strong feelings surface.

CARPE DIEM

Create an action plan for your next griefburst. For example, you might plan to drop whatever you are doing and go for a walk or record thoughts in your journal.

45.

PRAY.

• Prayer is mourning because prayer means taking your feelings and articulating them to someone else. Even when you pray silently, you're forming words for your thoughts and feelings and you're offering up those words to a presence outside yourself.

• Someone wise once noted, "Our faith is capable of reaching the realm of mystery."

• Did you know that real medical studies have shown that prayer can actually help people heal?

• If you believe in a higher power, pray. Pray for the person who died. Pray for your questions about life and death to be answered. Pray for the strength to embrace your pain and to go on to find continued meaning and life and living. Pray for others affected by this death.

• Prayer is a good way to mourn in the workplace. Find a quiet spot and dedicate a few moments to prayer. You may want to start every morning at work with a silent prayer. Or type up a short prayer and place it somewhere in your work space you'll see if often.

CARPE DIEM

Bow your head right now and say a silent prayer. If you are out of practice, don't worry; just let your thoughts flow naturally.

46.

WRITE DOWN YOUR "SOMEDAY I'M GOING TO..." LIST.

- Times of loss can be a good time to reassess what's really important to us. They're also a good time to take a good, hard look at the things we still want to accomplish in this short life.

- How many times have you said to yourself, "Someday I'm going to..." What are your "somedays"? Surf in Hawaii? Research your genealogy? Finish a college degree? Invite you neighbors over to dinner? Hike in the mountains of Colorado?

- At work, you may also have "somedays." Maybe you've always wanted to work in a different department, invite your coworkers to your house for dinner, or start a new career altogether.

- Write down your "somedays." Include little things and big things, personal things and work things. Then, after letting the list sit for a few days, pick it up again and cross off anything that deep down in your soul you don't really and truly want to do. (Remember—you can always add things to your list later.)

CARPE DIEM

Choose one thing from your "someday" list and take the first step to accomplishing it today.

47.

LAUGH.

- Humor is one of the most healing gifts of humanity. Laughter restores hope and assists us in surviving the pain of grief.

- Don't fall into the trap of thinking that laughing and having fun are somehow a betrayal of the person who died. Laughing doesn't mean you don't miss the person who died. Laughing doesn't mean you aren't in mourning.

- In the workplace, we're much more accepting of laughter than we are of tears, yet both are necessary expressions of our feelings. The next time you're enjoying someone's laughter, remind yourself that you should try to be just as open to her tears.

- I've heard it said that laughter is a form of internal jogging. Not only is it enjoyable, it is good for you. Studies show that smiling, laughing and feeling good enhance your immune system and make you healthier. If you act happy, you may even begin to feel some happiness in your life again.

CARPE DIEM

Memorize an appropriate joke to tell at work tomorrow.
Notice how your telling of it makes people feel.

48.

SURF THE WEB.

- The Web has a number of interesting and informative resources for mourners.

- Many articles about grief are available online. Most grief organizations (MADD, Parents of Murdered Children, American Association of Suicidology, Widowed Persons Service) now have Web pages.

- Search the word "grief" and see what you find. Use a more specific term (widow, homicide, etc.) if appropriate.

- If your workplace allows internet access, use a few minutes at work to search for grief resources.

CARPE DIEM

Sit down at your computer today and do a search. If you don't own a computer or have access to one at work, visit your local library. Don't forget to visit the Center for Loss Web site: www.centerforloss.com.

49.

THINK POSITIVE.

- After a death, it's normal—even necessary—to feel numb, depressed, afraid, angry and many other difficult feelings. Indeed, you must allow yourself ample time to acknowledge and experience your painful thoughts and feelings. Life will be hard for a while.

- But over time and with the love and support of others, your life can be happy again. You must trust in your ability to heal. You must trust that you will live and love fully again.

- Even in the midst of your grief, strive to think positive. Neuroscientists now understand that the human brain has the power to create its own reality. If you believe—really believe—that you can do something, you probably can.

- Visualize yourself nurturing a friendship or achieving a goal. Visualize yourself laughing and having fun. Visualize yourself at peace. You may not be able to live these realities today, but projecting yourself forward into a happier future may well help you achieve that future.

CARPE DIEM

What is most worrying you about the coming days or weeks? Close your eyes and visualize a positive outcome.

50.

TELL SOMEONE YOU LOVE THEM.

- Your loss has made you very aware of how love makes the world go 'round.

- Sometimes we love people so much, we forget to tell them "I love you." Or we (mistakenly) believe that they know they are loved, so we don't need to tell them.

- These three simple words have deep, spiritual meaning, yet we sometimes fail to see that until it's too late.

- At work, it's appropriate to tell others that they're special to you and that their friendship means a lot.

- My dad loved me, but it wasn't until just before his death that he whispered to me, "I love you." I miss you, Dad.

CARPE DIEM
Call someone you love right now and give them the
lasting gift of your words of love.

51.

SIMPLIFY YOUR LIFE.

- Many of us today are taking stock of what's really important in our lives and trying to discard the rest.

- You may feel overwhelmed by all the tasks and commitments you have. If you can rid yourself of some of those extraneous burdens, you'll have more time for mourning and healing.

- What is it that is overburdening you right now? Have your name taken off junk mail lists, ignore your dirty house, stop attending any optional meetings you don't look forward to.

CARPE DIEM

Cancel your newspaper subscription(s) if you're depressed by what you read. Quit watching TV news for a while.

52.

BELIEVE IN THE CAPACITY TO HEAL.

- All the veteran grievers I have ever had the privilege of meeting and learning from would want me to tell you this: You will survive.

- If your loss was recent, you may think you cannot get through this. You can and you will. It may be excruciatingly difficult, yes, but over time and with the love and support of others, your grief will soften and you will find ways to be happy again. There will come a day when the death is not the first thing you think of when you wake up in the morning.

- Many mourners also struggle with feeling they don't *want* to survive. Again, those who have gone before you want you to know that while this feeling is normal, it will pass. One day in the not-too-distant future you will feel that life is worth living again. For now, think of how important you are to your children, your partner, your parents and siblings, your friends.

- As time passes, you may also choose not simply to survive, but to truly live. The remainder of your life can be full and rich and satisfying if you choose life over mere existence.

CARPE DIEM

If you're feeling you won't make it through the next few weeks or months, talk to someone about your feelings of panic and despair. The simple act of expressing these feelings may render them a little less powerful.

53.

START A SUPPORT GROUP AT WORK.

- Grief support groups are a healing, safe place for many mourners to express their thoughts and feelings.

- Support groups help mourners know that they're not alone. Members both support one another and learn from each other. And support groups often develop into very tight-knit, loyal and lasting social circles.

- One way to mourn at work is to create a time and a place to do just that. A grief support group that meets once a week or twice a month at lunchtime is a good format. Ask your employer to consider bringing in a specially trained grief support group facilitator. (A training course for bereavement support group facilitators is offered through the Center for Loss; visit www.centerforloss.com for details.)

- If you are newly bereaved, you may not feel ready for a support group. Many mourners are more open to joining a support group 6-9 months after the death.

- *Bereavement Magazine* keeps an updated list of support groups throughout North America. Contact them at bereavementmag.com.

CARPE DIEM
Today, talk to several others in your workplace whom you know are struggling with a death. Ask if they'd be interested in forming a workplace grief support group.

54.

WALK AWAY.

- If you're at work and your grief grabs you, take its hand and go for a walk.

- If you can't concentrate on your work, don't sit at your desk feeling completely miserable. Instead, step outside into the fresh air and start walking.

- If you need to ask a supervisor's permission to leave your post, ask. A compassionate supervisor will understand that giving you a short break to take a walk is a far more effective use of resources than forcing you to call in sick.

- If you're feeling sad or fatigued, use your regular breaks throughout the day to walk. Force yourself out the door and onto the pavement for a few minutes. I guarantee you'll feel better.

- Walk briskly. You can walk off some of the intensity and energy of your emotions if you walk quickly and get your heart pumping and your muscles flexing.

CARPE DIEM
Get up right this minute and take a ten minute walk.

55.

GET AWAY FROM IT ALL.

- Sometimes it takes a change of scenery to reveal the texture of our lives.

- New people and places help us see our lives from a new vantage point and can assist us in our search for meaning.

- Often, getting away from it all means leaving civilization behind and retreating to nature. But it can also mean temporarily abandoning your environment and spending time in one that's altogether different.

- At work, get away from it all every few hours by getting up, walking around, looking out the window and getting a drink of water. Take a reflective "time out" for several minutes.

- When your time allows, consider really and truly getting away from it all. Visit a foreign country. Go backpacking in the wilderness. Spend a weekend at a monastery.

CARPE DIEM

Plan a trip to somewhere far away. Ask a friend to travel with you. Just don't do this too soon; running away is not the same as getting away.

56.

BREATHE.

- When you're at work and the demands of your job and the demands of your grief together feel overwhelming, stop what you're doing for a few minutes and breathe deeply.

- If you can, give yourself five full minutes to concentrate on your breathing. Breathe from your diaphragm; push your belly out as you breathe in and pull your belly in as you breathe out. Imagine that you're inhaling the spiritual energy you need to heal and that you're exhaling your sadness and bad feelings.

- Breathing opens you up. Grief may have closed you down. The power of breath helps to fill your empty spaces. The old wisdom of "count to ten" is all about taking a breath to open up space for something else to happen.

- Meditate if meditation helps center you. Find someplace quiet, be still, close your eyes and focus on breathing in and out. Relax your muscles. Listen to your own heartbeat.

- Consciously breathe in and out; you can slow the world down and touch the edges of your true self.

CARPE DIEM

Sit down, focus on something 10 feet away and take 20 deep breaths.

57.

LISTEN TO THE MUSIC.

- Many workplaces allow employees to listen to music throughout the day. If yours does, take advantage of this privilege by tuning into music that will help soothe your grieving heart.

- We all have certain musical likes and dislikes. Pay attention to which types of music make you feel calm, hopeful, and uplifted. Tune into these during the workday.

- Instrumental music is often a good fit for the workplace. It has no lyrics to distract your mind, yet its lovely melodies can help create a nice mood.

- Workplace studies have proven that the right music at the right volume can help people relax, focus more intently upon their tasks, absorb material and information at a higher rate, and be, in general, more productive.

CARPE DIEM

Play some music at work today. Choose something that
makes you feel calm and hopeful.

58.

TALK TO A COUNSELOR.

- While grief counseling is not for everyone, many mourners are helped through their grief journeys by a compassionate counselor.

- If possible, find a counselor who has experience with grief and loss issues. Look for certification from the Association of Death Education and Counseling (ADEC).

- Your employer's Employee Assistance Program, or EAP, may provide free or low-cost access to counseling. If you are fortunate to have access to this wonderful resource, take advantage of it.

- Your church pastor may also be a good person to talk to during this time, but only if she affirms your need to mourn this death and search for meaning.

CARPE DIEM

Contact your human resources department and learn more about your EAP counseling services or mental health insurance coverage.

59.

TAKE A MINI-VACATION.

- Don't have time to take time off? Plan several mini-vacations this month instead.

- What creative ideas can you come up with to renew yourself? Here are a few ideas to get you started.
  - Schedule a massage with a professional massage therapist.
  - Have a spiritual growth weekend. Retreat into nature. Plan some alone time. Go into exile.
  - Go for a drive with no particular destination in mind. Explore the countryside, slow down and observe what you see.
  - Treat yourself to a night in a hotel or bed and breakfast.
  - Visit a museum or a zoo.
  - Go to a yard sale or auction.
  - Go rollerskating or rollerblading with a friend.
  - Drop by a health food store and walk the aisles.

- Remember—you can have fun and grieve at the same time. Don't feel guilty for needing a break; it will help you survive and revive.

CARPE DIEM

Plan a mini-vacation for today. Spend one hour
doing something renewing.

60.

BELIEVE IN YOUR
CAPACITY TO HEAL.

- Set your intention to heal by making a true commitment to positively influence the course of your grief journey.

- You might tell yourself, "I can and will reach out for support in my grief. I will become filled with hope that I can and will survive this loss." Together with these words, you might form mental pictures of sharing your story with supportive coworkers and friends and seeing your happier self in the future.

- Setting your intention to heal is not only a way of surviving your loss, it is a way of actively guiding your grief. Of course, you will still have to honor and embrace your pain during this time, for this is a necessary step on the path to healing.

CARPE DIEM
Say these words aloud to yourself: Today I am filled with pain but there will be tomorrows in which I am filled with happiness.

WHEN YOU WANT TO HELP
SOMEONE WHO'S GRIEVING

A fundamental assumption of this book is that you *can* help someone who is grieving. While grief is an inner, spiritual journey in many respects, it needs to find outer expression. That's where you come in.

You can help by being a companion when the person who's grieving is ready to share his thoughts and feelings with another human being. You can listen without judging. You can hold him. You can spend time with him. You can help him with practical matters.

You can be there for him and offer him your ongoing compassion and empathy.

It's time that the workplace understood the value—the necessity—of reaching out to companion those who mourn. Thank you for helping create a work environment that realizes that people cannot be separated from their emotions and their spiritual struggles Monday through Friday from 8-5.

61.

ASK HOW YOU CAN HELP.

- If a coworker is grieving, ask how you can help.

- Don't take no for an answer right off. It could well be that your friend, like most of us, is having a hard time knowing how to accept help.

- Make a specific suggestion. Ask if you could run an errand or babysit the kids one evening. Ask if there are any household chores or maintenance issues that need to be taken care of.

- Assemble a crew made up of people at work who are willing to help with a project. Let's say your grieving colleague has a big yard; the volunteer crew could zip through his yardwork in one afternoon.

- If you know her well enough, drop by your coworker's house on a Saturday with a meal or with the intention to spend a few hours helping her do something that needs doing.

CARPE DIEM

Ask, "How can I help? Is there some practical way I could help you?"

62.

GET COMFORTABLE WITH ACKNOWLEDGING GRIEF AT WORK.

- We've already discussed how grief is part of the workplace and that the healthy expression of grief—even during the workday—is essential to healing.

- So if someone at work is grieving and maybe expressing that grief (mourning), what do you do? You acknowledge it.

- The worst thing you can do is ignore the griever. Resist what may be your natural impulse to look the other way when a coworker returns to work after a bereavement leave or pretend you didn't notice that a coworker's eyes are red from crying.

- Instead, acknowledge their grief. Tell him you're sorry. Ask her how she's doing. If it's appropriate, put your arm around his shoulders. Offer a tissue. Invite her to your desk or the breakroom for a cup of coffee.

- Look the person who is grieving in the eyes. Listen without judging or offering platitudes. Don't be the first one to walk away from the conversation.

- Other ways to acknowledge grief in the workplace include sending sympathy cards, giving flowers, attending the funeral, placing death notices/obituaries in your company newsletter, and simply being present to the person who is grieving.

CARPE DIEM

Tell someone who's mourning that you heard about the death and you're sorry. Then stand still and give the mourner a chance to open up to you a bit.

63.

PAY ATTENTION.

- Part of being a good grief helper is paying attention. We're trained to think that when we're at work, we need to be paying attention to our jobs. That's true. But to be compassionate, whole human beings, we also need to pay attention to the people around us.

- When someone in the workplace has suffered the death of a family member, pay attention. Listen and watch for cues that tell you he would (or would not) like your help.

- If you're getting the feeling he wants to talk, listen. If you're sensing he doesn't, don't push. If you're picking up signals that she's getting overwhelmed, figure out how you could make her life a little easier. And watch for the warning signs described in Idea 72.

- Of course, this doesn't mean you should wait for a "sign" to offer your help. You can and should offer your help regularly. But it does mean that by paying attention to your colleague's emotional "vibes," you will get better at knowing how and when you can really help.

CARPE DIEM

The next time you're at work, stop what you're doing and observe your coworker closest to you. Do her body language, facial expression and tone of voice reveal how she's feeling?

64.

ATTEND THE FUNERAL.

- Funerals are our way of saying goodbye to the person who died and honoring the life that was lived. They also mark the transition from life before the death to life after the death and activate our support systems. Meaningful funeral experiences create momentum to convert grief into mourning.

- Funerals are also our way of demonstrating support for those most impacted by the death. Even if you didn't personally know the person who died, it's appropriate for you to attend the funeral to show your support for a coworker. Make an effort to attend all the phases of the funeral—the visitation, the funeral itself, the committal and the gathering afterwards.

- In a compassionate workplace, policy allows everyone who wants to attend the funeral to be able to attend without penalty. If your company's policies make it hard for employees to attend funerals, talk to your human resource department about changing the policy. If it's not practical for everyone to attend the funeral, make sure your workplace sends at least one or two representatives.

CARPE DIEM

If the funeral was meaningful to you, let your coworker know. Many mourners feel comforted by the knowledge that it was a "good funeral."

65.

HELP WITH DETAILS.

- After a death, there are a multitude of details that must be attended to.

- Offer your help to those responsible for planning the funeral and burial.

- You could:
  - make phone calls to friends and relatives.
  - help write the obituary.
  - coordinate lodging for out-of-town guests.
  - set up the memorial fund.
  - track down necessary medical, insurance, and death benefit information.
  - select and work with the caterer.
  - find musicians for the visitation or funeral.
  - act as the liaison between the primary mourner and her boss.
  - galvanize workplace support.
  - run errands/do laundry/grocery shop.
  - and much more!

CARPE DIEM

Offer to help with the details. Be specific. Suggest a specific task you could accomplish or skill you have that may help.

66.

USE THE NAME OF THE PERSON WHO DIED.

- When you're talking to the grieving person about the death, don't avoid using the name of the person who died.

- To most mourners, your use of the name affirms their loss and lets them know you actually care. Hearing the name aloud also helps them feel the person who died isn't being forgotten.

- If you don't use the name of the person who died and instead use more generic terms, such as *your daughter* or *your husband*, you're making your interaction less personal and thus less supportive.

- But if you don't know the name of the person who died, it's definitely OK to use the generic term! It's always better to talk about the death than to not talk about it! And don't hesitate to ask the name of the person who died. Mourners often truly appreciate that you care enough to ask.

CARPE DIEM

Speak to someone who's mourning today and use the name of the person who died. See how the mourner responds.

67.

SEND FLOWERS.

- As a society, we have come to downplay the importance of flowers at the funeral. It's common to read in an obituary "In lieu of flowers, please contribute to the memorial fund..."

- But flowers are meaningful. They're beautiful and they smell good and they're present in a way that money can't be. They're tangible evidence of the love and support of others.

- Yes, flowers fade and die. They're ephemeral. But aren't all the best things in life?

- Sending flowers immediately after a death is a traditional way to show your support. Less traditional but just as effective is to send flowers later on, in the weeks or months after the death. Ask your coworkers to chip in to send flowers on the one-month anniversary of the death, for example.

- Keep in mind that there are cultural and ethnic rules to consider here. For Jews, for example, flowers are considered a symbol of happiness and are inappropriate after a death.

- Flowers in the workplace are a healing touch. Bring in a bouquet of fresh lilacs from home or surprise someone who needs it with an arrangement of cut flowers on her desk.

CARPE DIEM

Stop by the supermarket or nursery today and buy
an inexpensive flowering plant. Give it to someone who's
mourning to brighten his workspace.

68.

PLANT A GRIEF GARDEN.

- Did you know that gardening is the number one hobby in the US? I'll bet lots of your coworkers enjoy the physical labor—and spiritual rewards—of digging in the dirt.

- If your workplace has an outdoor space big enough for a flower garden, get permission from your employer, then, together with coworkers, plant a perennial garden. The garden can be planted in memory of someone who has died.

- A container garden—a grouping of potted flowers and plants—is a beautiful alternative.

- The garden can also be a healing place for mourners to spend time in quiet reflection. Some mourners might want to join you in planting and caring for the garden.

CARPE DIEM

Talk to a manager and find out how and where your
workplace could sponsor a grief garden.

69.

ESTABLISH A MEMORIAL FUND IN THE NAME OF THE PERSON WHO DIED.

- Sometimes bereaved families ask that memorial contributions be made to specified charities in the name of the person who died. This practice allows coworkers to show their support while helping the family feel that something good came of the death.

- You can also help establish a personalized and ongoing memorial to the person who died.

- What was meaningful to the person who died? Did she support a certain nonprofit or participate in a certain recreational activity? Was she politically active? Is there an organization that tries to prevent the kind of death she suffered?

- Your employer might provide matching funds, so don't forget to ask.

CARPE DIEM

Get together with a few people from your workplace and brainstorm a list of ideas for a memorial.

70.

ORGANIZE A TREE PLANTING.

- Trees represent the beauty, vibrancy and continuity of life.

- A specially planted and located tree can honor the person who died and serve as a perennial memorial.

- If your workplace has space to plant a tree, take up a collection to buy a tree from a local nursery and have it delivered. Then hold a lunchtime planting ceremony in which coworkers (including the person in mourning) roll up their sleeves, dig the dirt, and get the tree planted. You might also say a prayer or a few words after the tree is planted. Consider a personalized metal marker or sign, too.

- If enough money is raised, you could also buy a special bench and place it next to the tree. This will create a nice place to relax, converse, and even mourn, long into the future.

- For a more private option, get a group together to plant a tree in the yard of the grieving family. Consult your local nursery for an appropriate selection. Flowering trees are especially beautiful in the spring.

CARPE DIEM
Talk to a coworker today about organizing a tree planting
and see if you can get the ball rolling.

71.

COORDINATE WORKPLACE SUPPORT FOR SOMEONE WHO'S GRIEVING.

- In times of need, many people have an impulse to help but aren't sure how to go about doing it.

- Maybe you could coordinate support for a coworker who's grieving. Arrange for others to bring meals. Talk to your supervisor about allowing enough bereavement leave. Collect money for a memorial fund donation or flowers. Pass around a "thinking of you" card and have everyone sign it.

- If you know your grieving coworker well enough, you could also coordinate support for her outside the workplace. Talk to her neighbors or extended family about how they can help.

- Informally coach others in your workplace about how they can help the person who's grieving. Teach them some of the principles and ideas in this book.

CARPE DIEM

Write a "wish list" of ways people could help, then photocopy the list and distribute it widely. On the flyer, indicate that it would be helpful for people to call you and let you know which task they would like to help with so that efforts aren't duplicated.

72.

WATCH FOR WARNING SIGNS.

- Sometimes mourners fall back on self-destructive behaviors to get through this difficult time.

- Be aware of drug or alcohol abuse. Talk openly to the person who's mourning if you're concerned about such behaviors. Organize an intervention with other friends and family members if you need to.

- Pay attention to suicidal thoughts and feelings. Is the mourner isolating herself too much? Is she talking about suicide? Is she giving away possessions? Is she severely depressed?

- In the workplace, it's sometimes appropriate to report dangerous behaviors to the mourner's supervisor or the human resources department. They may be able to intervene in ways that could save a life.

CARPE DIEM

If the person who's mourning is being self-destructive, talk to another coworker right now and discuss your concern. Create a plan to supportively confront him.

73.

BRIGHTEN UP YOUR FRIEND'S ENVIRONMENT.

- Would the work area of the person in mourning benefit from a little sprucing up?

- Ask permission to paint her office in a fresh, new color. Paint is inexpensive and easy to redo.

- Or spruce up her work area with a new plant, a photo display, flowers, a new calendar, a pretty mug, etc.

- Together with some other friends from work, you might even volunteer to paint the mourner's kitchen or family room.

CARPE DIEM

Select one little project or item that will help make your friend's environment more pleasant or more soothing.

74.

DONATE A VACATION DAY.

- Some companies permit employees to donate vacation time to coworkers who are struggling with an illness or family crisis. If your company has such a policy, consider donating a vacation day to a coworker who's grieving.

- Ask others to do the same. Maybe with a little effort you can round up a whole week's paid leave. Just think what a difference a week off could make to someone who's really struggling.

- Sometimes people in grief *want* to work. They appreciate having a place to go and a routine to follow each day so they don't have to think so much about their grief. If you sense this is the case with the coworker you're concerned about, find a different way to help.

CARPE DIEM
Talk to your human resources person about donating a vacation day.

75.

JOIN TOGETHER.

- Part of the challenge with grief in the workplace is that it tends to isolate people. If people feel they need to keep their personal thoughts and feelings to themselves at work, they tend to withdraw—when what they really need is to reach out to others for support.

- Anything that helps coworkers join together is a good way to build relationships and help employees learn to support one another. Team-building exercises are one way, but there are many other less obvious ways, as well.

- Start a department softball team. Get involved in the Adopt-a-Highway program. Have a chili cook-off. Plan a company picnic. Hold a carwash that benefits a local nonprofit.

- Join together to support a cause—maybe even a cause that has something to do with the person who died. Walk a cancer walk together, or hold a vigil for our fallen soldiers.

CARPE DIEM

Make a list of group activities your department might be interested in.

76.

DON'T FALL BACK ON CLICHÉS.

- Mourners' deep and extremely complex feelings of loss are often dismissed with overly simple, empty phrases such as:
  - I know how you feel.
  - It was God's will.
  - Give it time.
  - You just need to keep busy.
  - Now she's in a better place.
  - Be strong.
  - At least he didn't suffer.
  - It's time to move on.
  - Try not to think about it.
  - Be glad you had him as long as you did.
  - She wouldn't have wanted you to be sad.
  - Life is for the living.

- Though well-intentioned, such clichés hurt because they diminish the mourner's feelings and take away his right to mourn.

- When you don't know what to say to someone who's grieving, just say "I'm sorry"—or refer to the list on the next page.

CARPE DIEM

Read Idea 77 right now. That way you'll be better equipped to talk to your friend next time you meet.

77.

DO SAY THIS.

- I'm sorry.

- I'm thinking of you.

- I want you to know I care.

- Lots of people here care about you.

- You are such a special person.

- I'm here for you.

- I'm a good listener.

- I want to help.

- I'm thinking of you and praying for you every day.

- I want you to know I cared about _____, too.

CARPE DIEM

Write a note or send an e-mail to someone who's mourning and let them know you're thinking about them. A handwritten note delivered in person to your coworker is the best option.

78.

WEAR A SYMBOL OF SUPPORT.

- In Victorian times, custom dictated that mourners wear black clothing for a certain period of time so that others would know they were in mourning. Wearing black armbands was another widespread tradition.

- These practices were helpful because they let the community know in a very visible way who needed support. They were also a reminder to the community that grief does not end after burial but rather extends far into the future—as does the need for support.

- A modern day example of this is sports teams whose players wear special numbers or black bands on their uniforms in memory of a team member who has died.

- If you are grieving or supporting someone who is, consider creating a symbol of support. If a child died, create and wear photo buttons in her memory. If a coworker died, maybe symbolic lapel pins could be distributed at work. If a coworker's wife died of breast cancer, pink ribbons could be displayed throughout the office.

- Be creative as you consider how to visibly demonstrate grief support in the workplace.

CARPE DIEM

Get together with a coworker today and brainstorm how to show your support for someone who is mourning.

79.

MAKE A MEAL.

- Often, people who are grieving don't have a lot of energy. It can be very hard to manage all the tasks of daily living—especially if the mourner is working outside the home.

- If you and perhaps some of your colleagues would like to help a coworker who's grieving, make a meal for her and her family. One person can make an entrée, one person could bring a salad, one person might bake cookies, and so on. Make big batches of everything so there will be leftovers.

- If you'd like to help more, arrange to supply a dinner once a week for a while. Solicit people in your workplace to contribute a one-dish meal.

- Sometimes the person you're trying to help will have a hard time accepting your kindness. We've all been trained to not lean on others, to try to gut it out ourselves. So if he protests good-naturedly, don't listen to him. Give him the meals anyway. He DOES need your help and he will appreciate it. If, on the other hand, he responds with anger (which can happen), that means he's really having a hard time accepting support from others and you may need to look for less overt ways to help.

CARPE DIEM

Leave a care package on the mourner's doorstep this weekend. Include a casserole, a salad, a dessert, and a card with a handwritten note of support. Make the note anonymous, if you wish, or sign your name.

80.

VISIT THE CEMETERY.

- Visiting the cemetery is an important mourning ritual. It helps us embrace our loss and remember the person who died.

- Memorial Day, Veteran's Day, Labor Day, Mother's Day and Father's Day are traditional days to visit the cemetery and pay respects.

- If the body was cremated, you may want to visit the scattering site or columbarium.

- If you are supporting someone in mourning, it's also appropriate for you to visit the gravesite and pay your respects. Let the person who's grieving know about your visit. Chances are he'll be touched by your show of support.

CARPE DIEM

If you can, drop by the cemetery today with a nosegay of fresh flowers. Scatter the petals over the grave.

81.

PASS AROUND A MEMORY BOOK.

- If a coworker has died, it's important to support his family as well as each other.

- A good way to pass along your support to the family is to compile a memory book.

- Buy a blank journal or scrapbook and pass it around, asking each person at work to fill in a page or part of a page.

- Write down a memory you'll always cherish about the person who died. Or fill a page with photos. Or write a note of support to the family. If you have an artist on staff, ask her to paint or draw a page for the book.

- Set a deadline for the pages to be completed so the book gets finished. Once it's ready, present it to the family in person.

- You'll find that not only is the family deeply touched by this sure-to-be-treasured memento, but that the act of writing or creating is healing for every person who participates.

CARPE DIEM

Buy a journal or scrapbook today and fill in the first page yourself.

82.

PLAN A COMPANY-WIDE IN-SERVICE ON GRIEF.

- Part of the challenge with grief in the workplace is that our society as a whole doesn't know how to handle grief and loss. Even in our own homes we're generally not very good at communicating about feelings of loss and expressing them in healthy ways.

- Hold a company-wide in-service on grief. Bring in a trained grief counselor who can give an insightful one-hour presentation to employees that covers what grief is (and is not) and how they can not only help themselves, but help coworkers who may be grieving. This same counselor may be able to give a different one-hour talk to HR and management about policy issues and appropriate modeling.

- You might also give out pamphlets about grief to all employees. For example, my Center for Loss has a brochure called "Helping A Friend In Grief" that is available in bulk and can be distributed affordably. The American Hospice Foundation (www.americanhospice.org) also has pamphlets available. (Or you could give copies of this book to everyone!)

- Use all your communication channels to help open up the discussion about grief. Put an article in your company newsletter. Create a bulletin board about do's and don'ts for helping someone in grief.

CARPE DIEM

Talk to someone in management or human resources
today about holding a grief in-service.

83.

LEAVE YOUR FRIEND ALONE.

- Sometimes the best way to help someone in mourning is to leave him alone for a while.

- Grief requires a natural turning inward, a contemplative posture of pondering the meaning of life and death.

- If someone in your workplace is mourning and rejects your offers of support, don't be hurt. Let him be for a while, then offer your presence and support in another week or two.

- Remember—some people, through no fault of their own, never learned that it's OK to need others, thus making it difficult for them to accept your active support. Some will keep you at arm's length.

- Also remember that people are often more receptive to your support 8-10 months after the death than they are early in grief.

CARPE DIEM
Just for today, set aside your worries for your friend. Enjoy your life.

84.

EARLY ON, REFRAIN FROM RELATING STORIES ABOUT SIMILAR DEATHS.

- Remember that this is a unique loss of a unique person. Especially early in your friend's grief, refrain from sharing similar types of stories.

- If your friend's loved one died of breast cancer, for example, refrain from talking about other breast cancer deaths you've heard about—unless your friend asks.

- If you have personally experienced a similar loss, it may be appropriate to share your story if and when the mourner is open to such dialogue. When you tell your story, be honest but also be hopeful. Aim to be a model of hope and healing.

- Never compare losses. No two deaths are ever mourned precisely the same. Don't offer judgments about which loss is worse.

CARPE DIEM

Gather information on local support groups that sound appropriate for your friend. Enclose this information in a card along with a supportive note.

85.

HELP THE PERSON WHO'S MOURNING MOVE TOWARD HIS GRIEF, NOT AWAY FROM IT.

- Our society teaches us that emotional pain is to be avoided, not embraced (especially at work!), yet it is only in moving toward our grief that we can be healed.

- Don't ask your friend how he's doing—ask him how he's *surviving*. This question calls for a more honest response.

- As you talk with him, remember this important helping principle: "Enter into what someone thinks and feels without thinking your job is to change what he thinks and feels." In other words, strive for active empathy.

CARPE DIEM

Write the person who's mourning a note reinforcing that you are there to listen to his thoughts and feelings, whatever they may be, and that you will never judge him. Encourage him to talk to you about his grief when he is ready.

86.

REMEMBER MOURNERS DURING THE HOLIDAYS.

- Mourners often feel particularly sad and vulnerable during Thanksgiving, Christmas, Hanukkah and other holidays they normally cherish. The holidays are all about spending time with the people we love—and when one of those people is no longer there, we feel our grief deeply.

- During your workplace holiday celebrations, be sensitive to the needs of those who mourn. They may not feel ready to participate in gift-giving and party-going. Ask before you assume they'd like to join in.

- This doesn't mean you should ignore mourners during the holidays, however. While they may not be ready for revelry, they may well need your presence. Offer to go out to dinner, just the two of you, or go to the movies.

- It may even be appropriate for you to invite your friend to share the holidays with you at our house or invite him on a trip during those times.

CARPE DIEM

Inquire about the mourner's holiday plans. Find a few hours to spend with him doing something he enjoys.

87.

LISTEN WITHOUT JUDGING.

- The most important gift you can give someone in grief is the gift of your presence. Be there for him. Initiate contact. And listen, listen, listen.

- Listen some more. If he wants to talk about the death over and over again, listen patiently each time. Telling and retelling the story helps mourners heal.

- Don't worry so much about what you will say in return. Instead, concentrate on the words being shared with you.

CARPE DIEM

Commit yourself to speaking with someone who's mourning within the next 72 hours. Promise yourself that you will focus on being the best possible listener. Keep in mind the 80/20 ratio: your friend should talk 80 percent of the time to your 20 percent.

88.

UNDERSTAND WHY LISTENING CAN BE DIFFICULT.

- Sometimes listening to someone in grief talk about her thoughts and feelings or recount the story of the death can be uncomfortable for us as friends and coworkers.

- It's no wonder it's uncomfortable. Our society doesn't understand the necessity of emotional and spiritual pain. We haven't been taught to embrace our pain so we can heal.

- Listening may stimulate unreconciled grief in us and demand exploration of our own pain and trauma.

- Listening to others struggle can also leave us feeling helpless and ineffectual.

- It is through being aware of our helplessness that we ultimately become helpful, however. Worry if you always think you know what to say. Remember—mouth closed, ears open. Just your quiet presence will be helpful.

CARPE DIEM

The next time you feel uncomfortable in the presence of emotional and spiritual pain, slow down and ask yourself why this is so.

89.

FOLLOW UP AND
FOLLOW THROUGH.

- Grief is a a long, wave-like journey—one that never really ends.

- People in mourning need our support in the days and weeks after the death but also in the months and years after the death.

- Don't wait for mourners to ask for help. You can be the one to offer.

- If you've promised something (e.g., "I'll stop by next week"), follow through. Now is not the time to allow yourself excuses.

CARPE DIEM
Record the anniversary of a workplace death in your
Palm Pilot or Daytimer. On the anniversary, be sure to
reach out to support those who mourn.

90.

GIVE YOURSELF A HAND.

- Being a good friend is an art few of us master. Being a good friend to someone in grief is especially hard.

- If you've been there for a grieving coworker, if you've been a companion through this most difficult of journeys, you are to be congratulated.

- Remember this: Even at work, it is the relationships in our lives that give our lives meaning. You have nurtured a caring, respectful relationship as well as helped another human being heal.

- Thank you for your compassion.

CARPE DIEM

As I pointed out early in this book, grief changes people. How have you been changed by the experience of supporting someone in grief?

WHEN THE WORKPLACE IS
AFFECTED BY TRAUMATIC DEATH

Sometimes a tragedy will affect an entire company or organization. I think of the companies affected by September 11, 2001—in particular Cantor Fitzgerald, the brokerage house with offices on the top floors of the North Tower. Of the 2,800 who died that fateful day at the World Trade Center, about one-quarter worked for Cantor Fitzgerald or its subsidiaries.

Similar but smaller-scale tragedies happen to companies more often than we think. Right here in Fort Collins, Colorado, where I live and have my Center for Loss and Life Transition, a real estate developer and two of his partners recently died together in a plane crash. Their small company was devastated by the deaths.

Other types of traumatic deaths that can complicate grief in a workplace include accidental deaths at work, military deaths, homicides, and suicides.

These types of deaths make blending work and grief a necessity. In these situations, there is no avoiding the fact that employees' grief must be responded to proactively and compassionately for months after the tragedy.

If your workplace has been affected by a traumatic death, read the following 10 ideas carefully then make a plan to help you and your colleagues through this extraordinarily difficult time.

91.

ALWAYS ERR ON THE SIDE OF COMPASSION.

- When a tragedy befalls your workplace, everyone is thrown into crisis mode. Decisions affecting people's health, livelihoods and well-being often must be made quickly.

- Now is the time to decide with your heart, not with financial, legal or practical considerations in mind.

- Do the right thing. If employees need medical help, get it for them. If they need mental health assistance or spiritual support (and they most assuredly will), get it for them. If they need time off or money, help them get it.

- Be a compassionate human being first and an employer or employee second. Help the people who need help in any way you can.

- How can I really help? That is the most important question you must ask yourself.

CARPE DIEM
It is said that you cannot control what happens to you—you can only control how you react to what happens to you. This is one of those times.

92.

MAKE A PLAN.

- When a tragic death impacts your workplace, the best place to turn would be your company crisis manual. Larger organizations often have written policies about how to handle crisis situations, during and after.

- If you don't have a crisis manual when a traumatic death occurs, pull together a team of key decision-makers immediately and craft a plan. Your plan should be compassionate and as thorough as possible. Who will need help immediately following the death? How will help be provided to them? Who will communicate with the press? Who will communicate with family members? What will happen tomorrow? And the next day? And the next?

- Enlist the help of as many people in your organization as possible in carrying out your plan. Many hands make light work. Plus, involving everyone is a way to help everyone integrate the loss into their lives and help your workplace heal.

CARPE DIEM
If you don't have a crisis manual or protocol, consider writing one now—before, I hope, you need it.

93.

REACH OUT FOR SUPPORT.

- If your workplace has been touched by a traumatic death, you must seek out special forms of help and support.

- Crisis debriefing by trained grief counselors is necessary in certain circumstances. If employees witnessed the death or have been affected by a violent death, this is essential.

- Ongoing grief counseling is almost always a good idea. Never assume that employees are handling the grief well on their own; always assume that structured grief support is the best practice in traumatic situations.

- As-needed, one-on-one counseling for workers most affected by the death is also a good standard of care. Consider making this available in addition to your normal mental health benefits.

CARPE DIEM

Contact mental health caregivers in your community and make a list of counselors who could provide crisis debriefing and grief counseling at your workplace if the need arose. Update this list annually.

94.

UNDERSTAND THE NATURE OF TRAUMATIC GRIEF.

- People who have been traumatized by a sudden and violent death have an especially difficult time acknowledging and absorbing the circumstances of the death itself.

- Sudden and violent deaths result in a kind of psychic injury and typically involve the creation of frightening and often intrusive thoughts about the distressful event that caused the death.

- Post-traumatic stress disorder, or PTSD, is a term used to describe the psychological condition that survivors of sudden, violent death sometimes experience. People with PTSD often have nightmares or scary thoughts about the terrible experience that they or someone they care about went through. They are often angry and anxious. People with PTSD need special help from trained counselors.

- In the early days after a traumatic death, mourners must first cope with the sudden and violent nature of the death. Only later on will they truly begin to cope with the fact that the person who died is gone.

CARPE DIEM

Determine if employees in your workplace may be suffering from PTSD and if so, what additional resources they may require. Talk to a trained counselor about this today.

95.

CREATE A "MOURNING ROOM."

- You may be familiar with the "crying room" at the rear of some churches. The soundproof room with large windows sits at the back of the sanctuary and is a place for mothers to bring their fussy newborns or rambunctious toddlers. There the children can cry (or the mothers can nurse in private) without disturbing the other worshippers, and the mothers can still see and hear (through a speaker system) and participate in the service.

- Some larger, more progressive companies have set aside nursing rooms for mothers to pump breast milk or nurse their newborns. Why not a mourning room for those who grieve?

- As I see it, this room would be a sanctuary for mourners to retreat to when they needed a good cry or some alone time during a busy workday.

- A mourning room (even a temporary one) could be equipped with books about grief and loss (including other types of loss, such as divorce, etc.), a daybed, Kleenex, a water cooler, a telephone. In addition to being used by mourners, it could be used occasionally by workers in any type of crisis or personal difficulty and for grief support groups and mental health education classes.

CARPE DIEM

Investigate the possibility of creating a mourning
room in your workplace today.

96.

CREATE A MEMORIAL WALL.

- Chances are, death will impact your workplace fairly regularly over the years. Last year a coworker buried a child; this year a manager was killed in a car accident. And next year? Next year will likely not be immune from loss, either.

- Death is a fact of life. Our culture is not very good at accepting this fact, but there it is. Death is just as much a part of life as birth.

- A good way to honor those who died as well as those who survive them is with a memorial wall. Dedicate an empty wall in your workplace to display photos of people who will be missed at the upcoming company picnic.

- Plan a display, or leave it up to employees to hang photos when they're moved to do so. If a coworker dies, you might frame her photo and caption it with her name, birth and death dates, and a sentence about her life. If a child dies, the mother can similarly hang his photo on the wall.

- If you place a console table against this wall, there will be a place to put flowers, a memory book, or other mementos when a death or tragedy occurs.

CARPE DIEM

If your workplace has been touched by tragedy,
begin planning your memorial wall today.

97.

PLAN A CEREMONY.

- I often say that when words are inadequate, have a ceremony.

- Ceremony assists in reality, recall, support, expression, transcendence.

- When personalized, the funeral ceremony can be a healing ritual. But ceremonies that take place later on can also be very meaningful. For example, a number of ceremonies have taken place at the site of the World Trade Center and ceremonies will likely continue to be held there on the anniversaries of the tragedy. Ongoing ritual helps you continue to both remember and integrate the loss into your head, heart and soul.

- If your organization has been affected by a traumatic death, you can hold a ceremony during the workday for all to attend.

- Ask a local clergyperson to help you plan and officiate the ceremony. It doesn't have to be overtly religious, but it should be spiritual.

CARPE DIEM

Have a ceremony for the person (or people) who died. It can be in addition to the ceremony held by the family, but do remember to ask the family if they'd like to attend.

98.

HOLD AN ANNUAL EVENT IN MEMORY OF THE PERSON (OR PEOPLE) WHO DIED.

- So that this special life will not be forgotten, and to demonstrate your organization's ongoing support, consider holding an annual event in memory of the person who died.

- Some groups hold an annual fundraising walk. Some gather for a picnic. Others have a golf tournament or a benefit concert.

- Your event could be more intimate if you'd prefer. Gather together the coworkers who were touched most deeply by the death and go out for lunch or dinner once a year, perhaps on or around the anniversary of the death.

- Annual events often become treasured traditions and provide a yearly dose of hope and healing.

CARPE DIEM
Begin planning an event, large or small, today.

99.

START A FOUNDATION.

- Some companies have charitable arms whose purpose it is to help employees in any kind of need.

- Levi Strauss has a foundation called Red Tab. Funded by the company as well as gifts from management, board members and employees, the foundation provides financial assistance to workers in times of need. Red Tab has also provided domestic violence education to Levi managers and money management education to employees.

- Your company could start a foundation to help families and employees affected by the tragedy. All it takes are financial gifts and the allocation of human resources to establish the foundation.

- The beautiful thing about a foundation is that it can give in perpetuity. While you may establish the foundation as a result of a specific tragedy, it can go on to help many more people in many ways into the future.

CARPE DIEM
Talk to an executive or board member today
about starting a foundation.

100.

LEVERAGE YOUR NEWFOUND UNDERSTANDING.

- Companies that endure a tragedy often emerge from the experience wiser and more compassionate. You have collectively learned what it means to grieve and mourn and, I hope, support one another in grief. You have learned that grief is inextricable from the workplace. You have learned that your work means so much more than the bottom line.

- After the crisis days have passed and your organization is well on the path to healing, take the time to institutionalize your newfound knowledge. That is, take the time to record what happened and what worked and didn't work in helping employees mourn.

- Now may a good time to revisit your company's mission and vision statements or rewrite human resource policies to ensure the continuation of a compassionate culture.

- Whatever you do, don't let your workplace forget all that it has learned from this tragedy.

CARPE DIEM

Task someone in your organization with the job of recording the lessons learned from this tragedy. Give her the time to complete this task thoroughly and expediently. Then take her report and make policy changes where appropriate.

A FINAL WORD

*"Not everything that is faced can be changed easily,
but nothing can be changed unless it is faced."*
— James Baldwin

My hope is that you agree with me that it is time to face the need for change in how we support grief in the workplace. Our efforts to both give and receive support in the workplace are not simply about helping each other adapt to changes and get "back to work." Our efforts to help must be anchored in genuine compassion for our fellow human beings.

My hope is that you will be able to apply many of the principles outlined in this book both in your "home life" and your "work life." Supporting one another in times of loss is not merely an opportunity to build relationships in times of shared grief; it is a responsibility to make our lives more compassionate, and the world a healthier place to live.

If you are in grief, allow me to remind you of the importance of self-care during this time. To be self-nurturing is to have the courage to pay attention to your needs, both at home and at work. Above all, self-nurturing is about self-acceptance. I plead with you to recognize it will take both time and a willingness to actively participate in the "work of mourning" before you again feel effective in your workplace. However, if you commit yourself to authentic mourning, you can and will go on to find meaning and purpose both at home and at work.

If you are supporting someone in grief, allow me to remind you that helping from the heart unfolds when we put aside our own life issues, if only for a moment, and just be there for another person. Yes, I know you come to work to "get things done," but if you have "companioned" a coworker in grief, you are to be congratulated. I thank you for making your workplace a more compassionate one. And, I'm sure your friend thanks you from the bottom of her heart, as well. As you truly help from your heart, you can and will experience a kinship with humanity. When you help from your heart, you are a part of love in action.

If you are an organization supporting an employee in grief, allow me to remind you that you are leading the way toward a more caring, supportive, life-enhancing work culture. You are among those employers who recognize that while work productivity is vital to your organization's future, compassionate caring is essential to your existence. Grief support is not always easy to achieve or measure, but the alternative is prohibitively expensive. Each and every day you must make a choice whether you will support employees in the workplace or whether you will not. The opportunity to choose is collectively ours, but the responsibility to act is personally yours. My hope is that this resource has helped you choose to reach out and support people who are in grief in your workplace.

MISCONCEPTIONS ABOUT GRIEF AT WORK

Please join me in helping dispel the following common (and harmful) misconceptions about grief at work.

Grief and mourning are the same thing.
Grief is what the griever feels on the inside. Mourning is the expression of those thoughts and feelings. Everyone grieves when someone loved dies, but if we are to heal, we must also mourn.

We only grieve and mourn the specific loss.
When someone we love dies, we not only mourn the loss of the physical presence of that person, but we also mourn other losses caused by the death, such as loss of security, loss of meaning in our lives, loss of part of who we are, etc.

Grief is an emotional response.
Grief affects our whole beings. So grief is not only an emotional response. It also affects us physically, cognitively, socially and spiritually.

Grief and mourning progress in predictable, orderly stages.
Grief is not predictable nor is it orderly. Grief occurs in a wave-like, non-sequential fashion.

"Grief work" should be done at home, in private.
It is impossible to turn emotions on and off and relegate them to home. We need to find ways to support grief in the workplace.

When grief and mourning are finally reconciled, they never come up again.
Grief never truly ends. We will always miss the people who have died and we will experience "griefbursts" now and then for the rest of our lives.

Only direct family members of the person who died grieve. When someone we care about dies, we grieve and we need to mourn, whether the person was a family member or not. The more deeply attached we were to the person who died, the more deep our grief will likely be.

Nobody, coworkers and employers included, can help you with your grief. The support of compassionate friends, coworkers and employers can and does make a significant difference.

THE MOURNER'S CODE

Ten Self-Compassionate Principles

Though you should reach out to others as you journey through grief, you should not feel obligated to accept the unhelpful responses you may receive from some people. You are the one who is grieving, and as such, you have certain "rights" no one should try to take away from you.

The following list is intended both to empower you to heal and to decide how others can and cannot help. This is not to discourage you from reaching out to others for help, but rather to assist you in distinguishing useful responses from hurtful ones.

1. **You have the right to experience your own unique grief.**
   No one else will grieve in exactly the same way you do. So, when you turn to others for help, don't allow them to tell you what you should or should not be feeling.

2. **You have the right to talk about your grief.**
   Talking about your grief will help you heal. Seek out others who will allow you to talk as much as you want, as often as you want, about your grief. If at times you don't feel like talking, you also have the right to be silent.

3. **You have the right to feel a multitude of emotions.**
   Confusion, disorientation, fear, guilt and relief are just a few of the emotions you might feel as part of your grief journey. Others may try to tell you that feeling angry, for example, is wrong. Don't take these judgmental responses to heart. Instead, find listeners who will accept your feelings without condition.

4. **You have the right to be tolerant of your physical and emotional limits.**
   Your feelings of loss and sadness will probably leave you feeling fatigued. Respect what your body and mind are telling you. Get daily rest. Eat balanced meals. And don't allow others to push you into doing things you don't feel ready to do.

5. You have the right to experience "griefbursts."

Sometimes, out of nowhere, a powerful surge of grief may overcome you. This can be frightening, but is normal and natural. Find someone who understands and will let you talk it out.

6. You have the right to make use of ritual.

The funeral ritual does more than acknowledge the death of someone loved. It helps provide you with the support of caring people. More importantly, the funeral is a way for you to mourn. If others tell you the funeral or other healing rituals such as these are silly or unnecessary, don't listen.

7. You have the right to embrace your spirituality.

If faith is a part of your life, express it in ways that seem appropriate to you. Allow yourself to be around people who understand and support your religious beliefs. If you feel angry at God, find someone to talk with who won't be critical of your feelings of hurt and abandonment.

8. You have the right to search for meaning.

You may find yourself asking, "Why did he or she die? Why this way? Why now?" Some of your questions may have answers, but some may not. And watch out for the clichéd responses some people may give you. Comments like, "It was God's will" or "Think of what you still have to be thankful for" are not helpful and you do not have to accept them.

9. You have the right to treasure your memories.

Memories are one of the best legacies that exist after the death of someone loved. You will always remember. Instead of ignoring your memories, find others with whom you can share them.

10. You have the right to move toward your grief and heal.

Reconciling your grief will not happen quickly. Remember, grief is a process, not an event. Be patient and tolerant with yourself and avoid people who are impatient and intolerant with you. Neither you nor those around you must forget that the death of someone loved changes your life forever.

SEND US YOUR IDEAS FOR
HEALING GRIEF AT WORK!

I'd love to hear your practical ideas for creating a more compassionate workplace. I may use them in other books someday. Please jot down your idea and mail it to:

Dr. Alan Wolfelt
The Center for Loss and Life Transition
3735 Broken Bow Rd.
Fort Collins, CO 80526
wolfelt@centerforloss.com

I hope to hear from you!

My idea:

_____

_____

_____

_____

_____

_____

_____

_____

My name and mailing/email address:

_____

_____

_____

_____

ALSO BY ALAN WOLFELT

UNDERSTANDING YOUR GRIEF
TEN ESSENTIAL TOUCHSTONES FOR FINDING HOPE AND HEALING YOUR HEART

One of North America's leading grief educators, Dr. Alan Wolfelt has written many books about healing in grief. This new book is his most comprehensive, covering the most important lessons that mourners have taught him in his three decades of working with the bereaved.

In compassionate, everyday language, *Understanding Your Grief* explains the important difference between grief and mourning and explores the mourner's need to gently acknowledge the death and embrace the pain of the loss. This important book also reveals the many factors that make each person's grief unique and the myriad of normal thoughts and feelings the mourner might have. Alan's philosophy of finding "companions" in grief versus "treaters" is explored. Dr. Wolfelt also offers suggestions for good self-care.

Throughout, Dr. Wolfelt affirms the readers' rights to be compassionate with themselves, lean on others for help, and trust in their innate ability to heal.

ISBN 1-879651-35-1 • 176 pages • softcover • $14.95

Companion
PRESS

All Dr. Wolfelt's publications can be ordered by mail from:
Companion Press
3735 Broken Bow Road • Fort Collins, CO 80526
(970) 226-6050 • Fax 1-800-922-6051
www.centerforloss.com

ALSO BY ALAN WOLFELT

THE UNDERSTANDING YOUR GRIEF JOURNAL
EXPLORING THE TEN ESSENTIAL TOUCHSTONES

Writing can be a very effective form of mourning, or expressing your grief outside yourself. And it is through mourning that you heal in grief.

The Understanding Your Grief Journal is a companion workbook to *Understanding Your Grief.* Designed to help mourners explore the many facets of their unique grief through journaling, this compassionate book interfaces with the ten essential touchstones. Throughout, journalers are asked specific questions about their own unique grief journeys as they relate to the touchstones and are provided with writing space for the many questions asked.

Purchased as a set together with *Understanding Your Grief,* this journal is a wonderful mourning tool and safe place for those in grief. It also makes an ideal grief support group workbook.

ISBN 1-879651-39-4 • 112 pages • softcover • $14.95
(plus additional shipping and handling)

Companion
P R E S S

All Dr. Wolfelt's publications can be ordered by mail from:
Companion Press
3735 Broken Bow Road • Fort Collins, CO 80526
(970) 226-6050 • Fax 1-800-922-6051
www.centerforloss.com

ALSO BY ALAN WOLFELT

THE JOURNEY THROUGH GRIEF:
REFLECTIONS ON HEALING
Second Edition

This revised, second edition of *The Journey Through Grief* takes Dr. Wolfelt's popular book of reflections and adds space for guided journaling, asking readers thoughtful questions about their unique mourning needs and providing room to write responses.

The Journey Through Grief is organized around the six needs that all mourners must yield to—indeed embrace—if they are to go on to find continued meaning in life and living. Following a short explanation of each mourning need is a series of brief, spiritual passages that, when read slowly and reflectively, help mourners work through their unique thoughts and feelings.

"The reflections in this book encourage you to think, yes, but to think with your heart and soul," writes Dr. Wolfelt. "They invite you to go to that spiritual place inside you and, transcending our mourning-avoiding society and even your own personal inhibitions about grief, enter deeply into the journey."

Now in softcover, this lovely book is more helpful (and affordable) than ever!

ISBN 1-879651-34-3 • 176 pages • softcover • $16.95
(plus additional shipping and handling)

Companion
PRESS

All Dr. Wolfelt's publications can be ordered by mail from:
Companion Press
3735 Broken Bow Road • Fort Collins, CO 80526
(970) 226-6050 • Fax 1-800-922-6051
www.centerforloss.com

ALSO BY ALAN WOLFELT

WHEN YOUR PET DIES
A GUIDE TO MOURNING, REMEMBERING AND HEALING

When your pet dies, you may struggle with your grief. You may feel overwhelmed at the depth of your sadness. This book affirms the pet owner's grief and helps you understand why your feelings are so strong. It also offers practical suggestions for mourning—expressing your grief outside of yourself—so that you can heal. Ideas for remembering and memorializing your pet are also included.

Dr. Wolfelt has been a dog lover and owner for a long time, suffering the loss of his Husky several years ago. Many have been asking Dr. Wolfelt to write a book about pet loss to add to his comprehensive list of publications about grief. Here it is—in his compassionate, practical, inimitable style.

ISBN 1-879651-36-X • 96 pages • softcover • $9.95
(plus shipping and handling)

Companion
PRESS

All Dr. Wolfelt's publications can be ordered by mail from:
Companion Press
3735 Broken Bow Road • Fort Collins, CO 80526
(970) 226-6050 • Fax 1-800-922-6051
www.centerforloss.com